COLLINS GEM
CATS

COLLINS GEM
Chinese

COLLINS GEM

GEM

COLLINS GEM
HORSES
& PONIES
a mine of information

COLLINS GEM
INSECTS
a mine of information

COLLINS GEM
KINGS &
QUEENS
a mine of information

COLLINS GEM
MUSHROOMS
& TOADSTOOLS
a mine of information

COLLINS GEM
SNAKES
a mine of information

COLLINS GEM
SPIDERS
a mine of information

COLLINS GEM
STRESS
Survival Guide
a mine of information

COLLINS GEM
TAROT
a mine of information

COLLINS GEM
WINE
Guide
a mine of information

COLLINS GEM
WORLD
atlas
a mine of information

COLLINS GEM
YOGA
a mine of information

COLLINS GEM
ZODIAC
Types
a mine of information

CARD TRICKS

The Diagram Group

HarperCollins*Publishers*

Many thanks to Isabella Percy and Toby Gee for testing the tricks

HarperCollins*Publishers*
Westerhill Road, Bishopbriggs, Glasgow G64 2QT

A Diagram book first created by Diagram Visual Information Limited of 195 Kentish Town Road, London NW5 2JU

Photography: PS5 Limited

First published 2001

Reprint 10 9 8 7 6 5 4 3 2 1 0

ISBN 0 00 712196-2

Printed in Italy by Amadeus S.p.A.

Foreword

Card tricks are the most popular of all magic tricks. You can take a pack of cards anywhere, and many tricks can be performed with just an ordinary pack and no other props.

Performing tricks with playing cards has been a popular pastime among young and old for as long as playing cards have been around – at least 700 years. Since that time people have been trying to bedazzle and astound others with their skill in tricking them with cards.

Collins Gem Card Tricks is a fascinating guide on how to perform over 60 card tricks. It starts with the basic card skills you need to develop, and gives advice on how to practise and develop a good performance. Also included is an easy-to-use glossary of important terms used in performing card tricks.

Each trick is described with step-by-step instructions, complemented by clear, explanatory illustrations. The tricks are arranged by type, in roughly ascending order of difficulty.

Created by the Diagram Group, the book is an attractive companion volume to the same team's *Collins Gem Card Games*.

4

Contents

Using this book

THE TRICKS
Each trick is described as follows:

> **Effect** – what the audience will see happen.
> **Equipment** – the materials you need to do the trick (it is assumed that a table or flat surface is available).
> **Preparation** – techniques you need to practise and any card sorting or prop preparation required.
> **Performing** – a step-by-step procedure (with illustrations) explaining how the trick is done.

Skill level
The tricks in this book are arranged into chapters according to the number and type of cards that are required, and whether any props are needed.

Within each chapter the tricks are arranged in terms of increasing difficulty, with simpler tricks at the beginning and harder tricks at the end. Some tricks are more suitable for older performers because of the skills required. Many of those in Chapter 4, involving sleights of hand, are of this type. Most, however, are appropriate for all age levels.

Props
Some tricks require special props. You can usually find these around the house – a handkerchief, for example, is used in several tricks. You might also need a particular item of clothing. Some tricks require the performer to wear a jacket with deep side pockets big enough to hide two packs of cards.

Introduction

CARDS

An ordinary pack of playing cards is made up of 52 cards: 13 cards – ace (A) to king (K) – in each of four suits (clubs, spades, diamonds, hearts). Most of the tricks in this book call for this type of ordinary pack. Some tricks require two ordinary packs.

A few tricks in this book require special types of packs or cards – such as the stripper deck, the Svengali deck, double-backed cards and two-sided cards. These can be purchased from magic and games shops.

A pack of playing cards also includes two jokers, which are set aside for most card games and tricks, although some of the tricks described here use the jokers.

CARD TYPES

Cards usually come in one of two sizes: bridge size, the standard size in the UK, and poker size (slightly wider). Either is suitable for card tricks.

Good cards are linen faced or plastic faced and wear well. They are made by well-known companies such as American Bicycle, DeLa Rue, Piatnik, TallyHo or Waddington. Avoid cheap paper cards.

Choose a pack that has a white border around the back pattern. This makes it easier to perform certain tricks, such as those where some cards are facing backwards in a pack.

CARD HANDLING

The tricks in this book are all easy to perform, but they do require practice at handling the cards. You will develop your card-handling skills gradually as you learn new tricks. Being able to handle cards well has many advantages. Your presentation looks much more professional and your audience takes you more seriously. Slick card handling is part of the entertainment – it can mesmerise your audience. Finally, and most importantly, good card handling is essential for the effective performance of many card tricks.

THE OVERHAND SHUFFLE

This is the most common way to mix up the cards. Modifying the way this is done is the basis of many tricks.

Nearly new cards
Most card tricks work better if the performer uses nearly new or little-worn cards. They are not as slippery as new cards, but they still have plenty of bounce and are not dog-eared or rough. Presentation can be much slicker using such cards.

● Hold the deck in the left hand gently between thumb and fingers, with the backs of the cards facing to your left (1).

1

2

- With the right hand, pick up a block of cards from the lower half of the pack (2).

- Bring this block of cards back over the top half of the pack.

- With the thumb of your left hand, scrape a few cards off the block and onto the pack, raising your right hand slightly as you do so (3). Repeat this action several times until you have shuffled all the bottom cards onto the top of the pack.

3

- Repeat the above procedure three or four times so that you have shuffled the entire pack.

- Practise this shuffle technique until you can do it smoothly, comfortably and without looking. You are then ready to modify the technique to perform some useful sleights of hand.

FALSE OVERHAND SHUFFLES

There are several ways of performing a false overhand shuffle. They achieve different effects.

Keeping bottom cards in place

Use this method when you have cards at the bottom of the pack which you want to keep there.

● Follow the normal procedure for the overhand shuffle, but instead of taking a block of cards from the bottom of the pack, take a block of cards from the top of the pack.

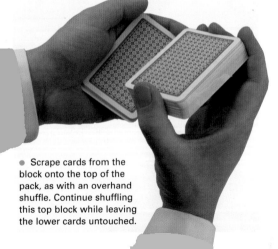

● Scrape cards from the block onto the top of the pack, as with an overhand shuffle. Continue shuffling this top block while leaving the lower cards untouched.

Keeping top cards in place

Use this method when you have cards at the top of the pack which you want to keep there.

● Follow the procedure for keeping bottom cards in place, but turn the pack around so that the cards are facing to your left, with their backs to your right.

● Shuffle as before while keeping the top cards (which are now at the bottom) in place.

Bringing top card to bottom

This method brings the top card to the bottom of the pack – it can be later brought to the top again if needed (*see over*).

● Hold the pack in the normal position for an overhand shuffle. With the left thumb, pull the top card off the pack and into the left hand.

● Now shuffle the rest of the cards on top of the first card in the normal way.

Bringing bottom card to top
This method brings the
bottom card to the top
of the pack – later it
can be brought to
the bottom again
if needed (*see
previous page*).

- Shuffle in the normal way as for an overhand
shuffle, bringing a block of cards from the
bottom of the pack and shuffling these on top
of the pack.

- As you shuffle to the end of the cards, scrape
them off singly. This is made easier by applying
pressure between the thumb and fingers of the
right hand and so bending the cards.

- The final card is then dropped on top
of the pack.

1

Keeping the order of the pack

You can give the impression of shuffling the pack while keeping the order of cards the same. This is particularly useful for tricks employing a stacked deck.

● Hold the pack in the left hand in the normal position for an overhand shuffle.

● With the right hand, pick up about half of the cards from the bottom of the pack.

● Drop these cards on top of the remaining cards in the left hand.

● Repeat this procedure several times. Done quickly and smoothly, it gives the appearance of shuffling, when really you are simply cutting the pack several times in quick succession.

THE RIFFLE SHUFFLE

This is an impressive and effective way of shuffling. Practise it until you can do it easily without looking at the cards.

● Cut the pack into two halves, with the top stack to your right (**1**).

2

● Place the two stacks together and at an angle so that when you riffle the two nearside inner corners with your thumbs, the two stacks interweave (2).

3

● When you finish riffling the cards, straighten them and square up the pack (3).

THE FALSE RIFFLE SHUFFLE

Like the overhand shuffle, the riffle shuffle can be
modified to perform various sleights of hand.

Keeping bottom cards in place

For a false riffle shuffle, you will need to adopt a more
crowded finger position than with the normal riffle
shuffle, so that onlookers can't see what is going on.

● Follow the normal
procedure for the riffle
shuffle, but release a
block of cards with
your left thumb before
releasing any cards
with your right thumb.

Keeping top cards in place

The procedure is the same as that for the false riffle
keeping bottom cards in place. The only difference is the
order in which you release the cards.

● Start by interweaving right and left piles as normal.

● Finish by riffling with your left thumb while holding
back the top of
the right stack, and
only letting
this group of
cards fall at
the end.

CARD SPREAD

Most card tricks are of the 'pick a card' variety. One of the best ways to present cards to a spectator is to spread the cards in the hand, either in a straight line or in a fan shape.

● Hold the pack face down in the left hand, as if you are just about to deal.

● Start pushing the cards into your right hand with your left thumb.

● Spread the cards in a rough line or fan supported underneath by the fingers of both hands, with the thumbs on top.

Ribbon spread

This is an on-the-table spread of cards. It is much easier to perform on a cloth-covered table than on a smooth, polished surface.

● Hold the squared-up pack face down between the thumb and fingers of your right hand.

● Place the pack on the table and sweep your hand from left to right, keeping your thumb and fingers in position and dragging your index finger across the top of the cards. Done smoothly, the cards will spread out neatly and evenly in a line.

Flourish

This is a quick and elegant way of exposing all the cards face up.

● After you have performed a neat ribbon spread (*see bottom of page*), rest your right hand at the end of the spread.

● With your left hand, flip over the left side of the left-hand card. A chain reaction will cause all the cards to turn over in a wave-like motion from left to right. Your right hand supports the last few cards as they turn over.

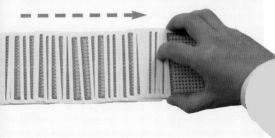

CUTTING THE CARDS

Cutting involves dividing the pack into two and putting the bottom half on the top. It alters the start and end point of the pack, but it does not alter the order or sequence of the cards.

The easiest way to cut cards is on a table top.

- Simply lift the top half of the pack (**a**) and place it to one side (**1**).

- Then place the bottom half (**b**) on top (**2**).

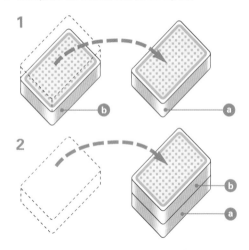

Swing cut

This is a much more elegant method than the basic cut (*see opposite*). It is done in the hand.

1

2

● Hold the pack face down by its short edges with your right thumb at the bottom left corner and your right index finger at the top left corner (1).

● With your index finger, lift and swivel the top half of the pack to the left, using your thumb as a pivot (2).

● Take the top stack in your left hand (3) and with your right hand bring the bottom stack over the top to rest on it. You have completed the cut.

3

False cut

This keeps the bottom card in place while the pack appears to be cut normally.

● Hold the pack lengthways between the fingers and thumb of the left hand.

● For a normal cut, grasp the lower half of the pack with the right hand, withdraw this bottom stack and bring it to the top.

● To make this into a false cut in order to keep the bottom card in place, follow the above procedure but squeeze the pack gently with your left hand as you withdraw the lower stack. This keeps the bottom card in place while the stack is withdrawn.

● Carefully shield the cards with your hands while you carry out this manoeuvre. This prevents the audience seeing exactly what is happening.

GLIDE

This sleight enables you to keep a selected card – one that you have already identified, for example – at the bottom of the pack so that you can produce it at any time.

- Transfer the selected card to the bottom of the pack using a false shuffle or some other technique.

- Hold the pack in your left hand, face down, with your fingers over and around the cards.

- With your little finger, draw back the bottom card a couple of centimetres. Now when you take cards from the bottom of the pack, you will avoid the selected card, which will remain on the bottom.

- Whenever you wish to take out the selected card, simply move the card forward into position with your little finger (**1**), then withdraw it from the pack as normal (**2**).

1

bottom view

2

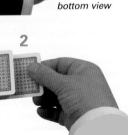

GLIMPSE

There are two effective ways of glimpsing the bottom card of the pack.

● In one case, simply take the pack in your right hand and square it against the table with the cards facing left (1). A quick downward glance is all that is needed to glimpse the bottom card.

● In the other case, grasp the pack in your right hand, with thumb underneath and fingers on top.

● As you transfer the pack from right to left hand, tilt the pack just enough to catch a glimpse of the bottom card (2).

Both techniques work well when you are taking the pack from a spectator just after she has shuffled it.

THE DOUBLE LIFT

Here, you take two cards from the top of the pack but give the appearance of taking only one. This has to be done cleanly, without fumbling, if it is to fool the audience.

● While you are talking and looking at the audience, square the deck with the fingers of your right hand.

● As you do so, bend your index finger and press it down on the top of the pack, and then lift the near ends of the two top cards with the ball of your right thumb.

● Move these two top cards very slightly to the right, and leave them there with your right thumb in place (1).

● Later, when you show the top card, it is easy to pick up the top two cards as one. Simply bend them up at the back as you did before and lift them cleanly off the top (2) and show them to the audience (3).

When you normally pick up a single top card, make sure your moves look the same. From the spectator's point of view, taking one or two cards from the top should look exactly the same.

THE SLIP FORCE

The success of some tricks depends on your being able to 'force' an unsuspecting spectator to pick a card you have already selected. Here is one force involving a simple sleight of hand,

which 'forces' the spectator to choose the top card of the pack.

● Stand with your right side to the audience with the cards in your left hand, furthest from the audience. The card you wish the spectator to have is on top of the pack.

● Riffle through the pack with your left thumb and ask a spectator to say 'stop' when she chooses.

● When stopped, tilt up the top cards using the right hand (1).

● Explain to the spectator that she has freely chosen a card. While you are doing this, press on the edge of the top card with your left fingers and in a sweeping motion remove the top pile with your right hand.

The top card – trapped by your left fingers – will drop down onto the lower pile (2). Done correctly, the sleight, in particular the sweeping right hand, both misdirects the audience and obscures the secret move.

- You now offer the spectator the lower pile and ask her to take the 'top' card. The card she has apparently 'chosen' from the middle of the pack is, of course, the card from the top.

THE PALM

Palming is the process of hiding a card in the hand. It is quite hard to master at first, but is a very powerful technique. Here is one way to do it.

- With the chosen card on top of the pack, and with the pack in your left hand as though you are about to deal, bring your right hand over to take the pack. As you do so, misdirect the audience in some way – perhaps with a long-winded explanation – and use your left thumb to push the top card to the right (1).

● With the middle fingers of your left hand, push the top card into your right palm. Providing you keep your right hand relaxed, you will find it folds easily around the card, and the move will not be conspicuous (2).

2

bottom view

● You can now take the pack back into your left hand, as though you have just changed your mind. Your right hand should hang naturally down by your side with the card hidden.

● Some time later you can retrieve the card – perhaps by appearing to pluck it from behind someone's ear.

● Practise palming in front of the mirror to ensure that your hand looks natural and no edges of the card can be seen.

SWITCHING PACKS

Many startling tricks can be performed by secretly exchanging a pack that has been shuffled for one that has been prearranged. To the onlooker, miraculous tricks are performed with an apparently well-shuffled deck.

Equipment

You will need to use two ordinary packs of playing cards of identical design, and an elastic band. You will also need a jacket with deep side pockets.

- Place an elastic band (**1**) around one end of the prearranged pack in order to hold the pack in place.

- Place this pack in the side pocket of your jacket.

- Use the unarranged deck to perform tricks described elsewhere in the book.

- When you are finished, have a spectator thoroughly shuffle this pack.

- Put the pack in your pocket (next to the prearranged pack), pretending that you have finished with it and are about to do something else.

- Grasp the second pack in your pocket and push the elastic band off with your thumb. Suddenly pretend to remember that you want to do another card trick.

- Bring out the prearranged deck. If you do this casually, the spectators will not suspect that the shuffled pack has been switched for another one.

PREPARATION

Simply knowing how a trick is done and how to carry it out will not make you a successful performer. You are still only halfway there. You need to entertain the audience and convince them – by all your actions – that something exciting is happening. This takes practice – and a lot of it.

Here are the dos and don'ts of preparation for mastering each trick.

Dos

- Learn one trick at a time.

- Learn the trick thoroughly so that you are absolutely confident about how to present it.

- Learn a few tricks well, rather than many tricks sloppily.

- Try a new trick on friends or family and listen to their comments.

- Track down the weak spots in a trick and work out ways to get around them, using misdirection if necessary.

- Practise frequently but in small doses. You are more likely to overcome a problem when you come to it afresh.

- Imagine what the trick will be like from the audience's point of view. Will it be interesting? Will they spot something they aren't meant to see? How can you distract them so they won't notice what you're doing with the cards? How can you finish the trick in a dramatic way?

- Continue working on a trick, making adjustments, until you are completely happy with it. This may mean the trick is slightly different to the way it is described here – but you will have made the trick your own.

- Make the props yourself or buy them from a reputable dealer in magic equipment. You can then be sure you are buying reliable equipment which looks good, does the job and will last.

- Remember, first and foremost, you are an entertainer – you must make your performance interesting and lively.

There is a saying among magic-trick performers: 'Practise. Practise again. Practise until you can do it perfectly. Then practise some more.'

- Adjust your finger positions if you find a particular move difficult or awkward – not everyone's hands are the same.

- Practise in front of a mirror. It helps 'fine-tune' your performance and allows you to see how it looks from the audience's point of view. It also encourages you to look away from your hands and at the audience.

DON'TS

- Don't show any trick until you have practised it thoroughly.
- Don't perform a trick until you can do it so well that you don't have to worry about 'what comes next'.

- Don't tell anyone how the trick is done.

PERFORMING

A performance of card-trick magic – whether a single trick or a whole routine – is not merely a collection of bits cobbled together. You need to prepare your performance as a whole piece, with a start and finish. Think through your act carefully so that it is smooth and polished and so that one trick or part follows on naturally from another.

THE STRUCTURE OF A PERFORMANCE

If you plan to do a performance, make your act last 10–15 minutes using six to eight tricks. Here are some suggestions as to what you might include:

● At the beginning do quick and easy tricks which allow you to relax and let the audience get to know you. Simple key card and mathematical tricks are suitable here.

● In the middle of the performance, when you and the audience are more relaxed, use longer, more complicated tricks which involve the spectators more. Tricks using arranged cards, sleights of hand or props are suitable here.

● Try to finish on a spectacular visual trick. The Fabulous Four Aces (*see page 140*), Three Cards Across (*see page 135*), and Finale (*see page 190*) are good tricks with which to finish your act.

Here are the dos and don'ts in preparing and performing your act.

DOS – PREPARING THE PERFORMANCE

● Choose tricks which are suitable for the kind of audience you expect.

● Read about magic and magicians, and use every opportunity you can to look at magicians as they perform and to learn from them.

● Plan your performance in detail.

● Decide in which order you are going to do the tricks, and how one trick will lead on to the next.

● Inject variety into your act. To the performer, the tricks work in different ways. To the spectator, most tricks appear to be of the 'spectator takes a card and the performer identifies it' type. Make sure that you emphasise the differences between each of the tricks and include a variety of tricks that involve more than one person, where cards are revealed in different ways, and where various props are used.

● Work out what to say from start to finish.

● Vary the pace of your performance; for example, intersperse slow tricks with fast ones.

● Be aware of your own strengths and weaknesses and tailor your performance to make the most of your strengths.

● Make sure your hands and fingernails are clean, and that you are neat and well groomed.

● Make sure you have all your props in the right places at the start of a performance.

● Expect to get excited and anxious before a performance. Even professionals do.

● Practise regularly and pay attention to detail. This increases confidence in your performance and reduces the chances of getting stage fright – an attack of nerves on stage.

● Take a dozen deep breaths before walking on stage. It calms your nerves and allows you to concentrate on entertaining your audience.

DOS – DURING THE PERFORMANCE

● Choose a trick you can do well as your first number.

● Speak clearly and talk slowly.

● Tell a story, make a joke – above all, entertain – but do it naturally. Be yourself. Find your own style.

● Be prepared to make changes during the performance if things go wrong.

● Use your hands and eyes to direct the audience where you want them to look.

● Use explanations and patter to misdirect the audience from what you are actually doing.

● Handle props confidently and openly to allay the suspicions of the audience.

● Involve spectators in the trick. This helps to direct attention away from yourself and whatever you are doing.

● Ask a spectator to show the chosen card to someone else in the audience. This prevents the possible embarrassment of the spectator later forgetting the card, or even purposely naming another card to spoil the trick.

● Relax and smile. Look as though you are enjoying yourself.

● React to your own tricks. Scratch your head, shrug your shoulders, and so on to help convey your feelings.

● Use words to create drama. Talk slowly to show concentration and build up suspense. Talk louder and faster at the climax of a trick.

● Think about the performance and strive to improve your presentation.

● Aim to make the audience believe – by your words, movements and appearance – that you are truly a successful magician.

● Leave the audience wanting more.

DON'TS – DURING THE PERFORMANCE

● Don't do two similar tricks in the same performance.

● Don't repeat a trick.

● Don't include too many 'take-a-card' tricks.

● Don't try to do a trick if you are not confident about it – you are likely to give a poor erformance.

● Don't speak too fast – easy to do if you are nervous. Slow down.

● Don't state the obvious, such as 'Here is a pack of cards.'

● Don't say anything to arouse suspicions, e.g. 'This is a pack of cards – look, there's nothing wrong with them.'

● Don't spoil a surprise by stating what will happen before it does.

● Don't insult anyone – whether present or not.

● Don't take everything so seriously that if things go wrong your act falls apart. Laugh with everyone else and then get on with the next trick.

GLOSSARY

backpalm A sleight (see *sleight*) that conceals a card behind the fingers of one hand.

block of cards A section of the pack kept together during shuffling, cutting or dealing.

cut Dividing the pack in two and putting the half that was on the bottom on the top. A deck can be also cut into several parts.

deal The method by which single cards are distributed from the top of the pack.

deck or pack Playing cards used for a particular game. The standard deck is 52 cards, i.e. four suits of 13 cards each.

double lift A sleight (see *sleight*) where two cards are lifted from the pack but the audience believes that only one card has been removed.

false count A count of cards which appears genuine but where the number of cards counted is really more or less than it appears to be.

false shuffle An apparently fair shuffle that keeps the cards in a set order.

fan Spreading the cards to form a neat fan shape.

finale The finish to a trick or an act – usually the high point of the performance.

fingerpalm Concealing a card between the fingers.

flourish A dramatic way of turning a spread of cards face up in a wave-like action.

force To give a spectator an apparently free choice but really making him or her select a predetermined card.

glide A sleight (see *sleight*) in which the performer retains the bottom card of the pack and deals the next card as if it were the bottom card.

glimpse To secretly view a card, usually the one on the bottom of the pack.

key card A known card which locates or marks the position of other cards.

misdirection The art of drawing the spectator's

attention away from a
secret move.

move The execution of a
sleight (see *sleight*) or
other secret movement.

overhand shuffle The
standard method of mixing
a pack of cards.

pack See *deck*.

palming Concealing a card
in the palm of the hand.

patter The storyline, jokes
or other talk used by a
performer during an act.

pile A portion of the pack
formed, for example, by
cutting the cards.

props Objects other than
cards used by a performer.

riffle To flick the edge or
corner of a pack to make a
clicking noise.

riffle shuffle An on-the-
table shuffle in which the
two halves of the pack are
interwoven as the thumbs
riffle and release the cards
singly at speed.

routine The order of
events that make up a trick
or a series of tricks in a
performance.

shuffle To mix the cards,
by hand.

sleight A skilful
movement of the fingers
by which a trick effect is
accomplished.

sleight of hand The
performing of sleights (see
sleight).

spread Cards in an
overlapping arrangement
which allows an individual
to easily pick a card or – if
the cards are face up – to
see the values of the cards.

squaring the pack Neatly
aligning the cards, e.g. by
tapping their edges on a
table.

stack An arrangement of
cards in a known or
predetermined sequence.

steal To secretly remove
something from the place
where it is concealed.

suits Clubs, spades, hearts
and diamonds.

switch To secretly
exchange one card for
another.

top The part of the pack
that is uppermost when
the pack is face down. The
'top' of a face-up pack,
therefore, is at the bottom.

1. Tricks using key cards

A 'key' card is a known card which you can place next to or near an unknown card to identify the location of the unknown card. When you find the key card, you find the unknown card.

THE MAGIC TOUCH

This trick requires at least two spectators.

PERFORMING

● Ask for a volunteer. As the volunteer comes forward, openly scan the cards. Say you are checking to make sure they are all there, but as you do so, glimpse the card at the top of the pack (**1**). This is the key card (**a**).

● Close the pack and place it face down on the table.

● Ask the volunteer to cut a small pile of cards (**2**) (**b**) from the top of the deck (**c**) and to memorise the bottom card (**d**).

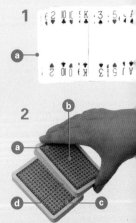

EFFECT
A spectator chooses a card from the pack. The card is returned to the pack and the pack is cut. The performer spreads the cards face up in a row and finds the card by apparently sensing reactions in the spectator.

EQUIPMENT
An ordinary pack of playing cards.

PREPARATION
The trick depends on the use of the glimpse (*see page 22*) with the top card as key.

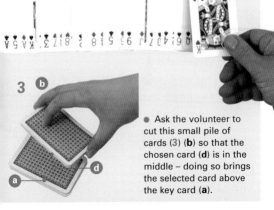

3

● Ask the volunteer to cut this small pile of cards (**3**) (**b**) so that the chosen card (**d**) is in the middle – doing so brings the selected card above the key card (**a**).

● Ask a second spectator to lift up some of the cards in the remaining pack (**c**). The volunteer then places the small pile (**b**) on top of this pack, and the spectator returns the remaining cards to the top of the pile, so losing the chosen card in the centre of the pack (4).

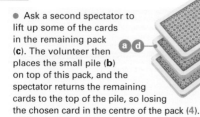

● Pick up the cards and turn them face up on the table, spreading them across the table so that most of them can be seen. The selected card will be directly to the left of the key card.

● Take the volunteer's arm and, starting at one end of the spread cards, pass the volunteer's index finger over the cards apparently sensing for small muscle reactions (5). Pass back and forth several times, and finally push the volunteer's hand forward so that the index finger touches the selected card. Say: 'This is the one; I can sense your reaction.'

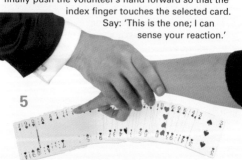

GET TOGETHER

EFFECT
The pack is cut in two, and the spectator and performer each take half a pack. They both choose a card from their respective piles, look at them and return them. When the piles are combined the two selected cards mysteriously come together.

EQUIPMENT
An ordinary pack of playing cards.

PREPARATION
The trick depends on the use of the glimpse (*see page 22*) with the bottom card as key.

PERFORMING
● Allow a spectator to shuffle the deck and cut it in half.

● Get the spectator to give you one half of the pack and to keep the other half.

● Each of you shuffles your pile of cards.

● Ask the spectator to remove any card from her pile, look at it and remember it. Say that you will do the same.

● Look at the card you have selected but make no attempt to remember it. Instead, glimpse the bottom card of your pile. This will be the key card (**c**).

● (1) Each of you places your selected card (**d**) on top of your pile (**a** and **b**).

● (2) Now place your pile (**a**) on top of your spectator's (**b**). Doing so puts your key card (**c**) on top of her card (**d**).

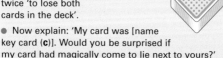

● Ask the spectator to cut the deck twice 'to lose both cards in the deck'.

● Now explain: 'My card was [name key card (**c**)]. Would you be surprised if my card had magically come to lie next to yours?'

● Hand the cards to the spectator. When the spectator sorts through them she will find her card next to yours.

TURN-AROUND CARD

EFFECT
A spectator selects a card from one of three piles. The performer merges the piles, attempts to find the chosen card and leads the spectator into thinking a mistake has been made. The performer then turns the tables on the spectator, suddenly exposing the right card.

EQUIPMENT
An ordinary pack of playing cards.

PREPARATION
The trick depends on the use of the glimpse (*see page 22*) with the bottom card as key.

PERFORMING
- Spread the cards face up to show the audience that the cards are well sorted.

- Re-form and cut the pack.

- Square the pack, and as you do so glimpse and memorise the bottom card. This is the key card.

- Place the pack face down.

- Ask a spectator to cut the deck into three even piles and take a card from the middle of any pile. (You should have followed which of the three piles has the key card at the bottom.)

- The spectator should then replace the chosen card at the top of any pile.

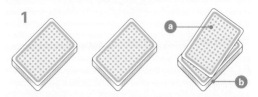

● (1) If the spectator puts the chosen card (**a**) on top of the pile containing the key card (**b**), ask him to cut that pile and replace the cut. This will put the key card on top of the selected card. Then put the piles together.

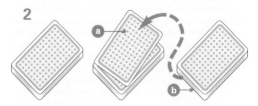

● (2) If the spectator places the chosen card (**a**) on a pile other than the one containing the key (**b**), put the piles together so that the key card goes on top of the selected card.

● Turn the pack face up and cut it into three piles.

● Spread each pile to show the spectator all the cards (**3**, opposite).

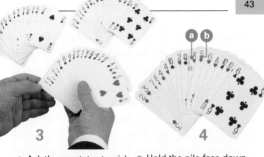

3

● Ask the spectator to pick out the pile containing the selected card.

● Pick up this pile (**4**). By this time you will have seen the key card (**b**) and know that the card next to it is the selected one (**a**).

● Hold the pile face down and start to deal the cards slowly face up on the table, overlapping each card.

● When (**5**) you deal the key card (**b**), note the card that follows it – this is the chosen card (**a**). Deal a few more cards.

● Now say that the next card you turn over will be the chosen one. Since the spectator saw you deal his card already, he will assume that you missed it.

● Pick up his card and turn it face down.

5

IN BETWEEN

You will need three or more spectators.

EFFECT
Two spectators each select a card from the pack. A volunteer then selects a card. They return the cards to the pack and the performer then extracts the volunteer's card sandwiched between the two spectators' cards.

EQUIPMENT
An ordinary pack of playing cards.

PREPARATION
This trick relies on the use of the glimpse (*see page 22*) and the bottom card as key. It also requires the ability to cut cards with precision.

PERFORMING
● Ask two spectators each to select a card from a shuffled pack.

● Get them to replace the two cards on top of the pack.

● Square the pack and as you do so glimpse and remember the bottom card. This is the key card (**a**).

1

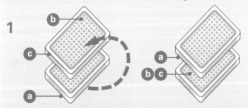

● Cut and replace the pack (**1**) so that the key card (**a**) is now on top of the two chosen cards (**b** and **c**).

● Ask a volunteer to name a card (not one of the spectators' chosen cards).

● Ask the volunteer to help you find that card. Get her to turn the pack face up and look for the card (**2**). You are looking for your key card (**a**). The spectators' cards (**b** and **c**) are next to it. The volunteer now takes out her card (**d**).

● As you bring the cards together to re-form the pack (**3**), slip your right little finger between the spectators' cards (**b** and **c**). Turn the cards face down and in the same movement cut the pack at the break where your little finger is inserted.

One card (**b**) goes
to the bottom of the
pack (**4**) and the
other (**c**) goes to
the top.

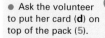

● Ask the volunteer
to put her card (**d**)
on top of the pack (**5**).

● Now cut and re-form the
pack (**6**) so that the bottom
card (**b**) rests on top of the
volunteer's card (**d**),
sandwiching it between the
spectators' cards (**b** and **c**).

● Ask the spectators to name
their cards. Thank the
volunteer for helping you find
their cards.

● Spread the deck face up
(**7**). The cards on either side
of the volunteer's card will be
the spectators' cards.

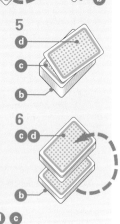

THE TWO DETECTIVES

This trick can be used to tell a story.

EFFECT
A spectator chooses a card and returns it to the top of the pack. The performer takes out the two black Js from the pack – the 'detectives'. By quickly manipulating the pack behind the back, the performer miraculously sandwiches the chosen card between the two Js – the detectives have found the card.

EQUIPMENT
An ordinary pack of playing cards.

PREPARATION
The trick depends on the use of the glimpse (*see page 22*) and the bottom card as key. You will need to practise manipulating the cards behind your back.

PERFORMING
● Ask a spectator to shuffle the pack.

● Take back the pack and square it, glancing at the bottom card as you do so.

● Ask the spectator to choose a card and place it on the top of the pack.

● Cut and re-form the pack (**1**), bringing the bottom card – the key card (**a**) – on top of the chosen card (**b**).

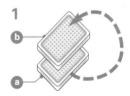

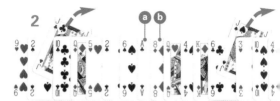

- Turn the deck of cards over and spread them out (**2**). Explain that you are looking for the two detectives – the black Js – who will help you find the card. In fact you are looking for your key card (**a**) which is to the left of the chosen card (**b**).

- Take out the two black Js and put them to one side.

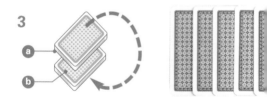

- Now cut and re-form the pack (**3**) so that the key card (**a**) goes to the bottom of the pack. The selected card will now be at the top of the pack (**b**).

- Tell the spectator: 'I'll let the detectives find the card.' With one hand place the deck behind your back. With the other hand, take one of the black Js and

place it face up under the top card (**b**) of the deck. Then take the other black J and place it face up on top of the deck (**4**).

● Cut and re-form the deck to hide the cards in the middle.

● Bring the deck round to the front and ask the spectator for the name of the chosen card.

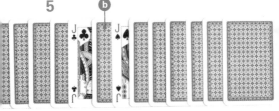

● Place the deck on the table and with a flourish spread the cards face down (**5**). The two black Js will be face up on either side of a card. The card sandwiched between the two is the spectator's card (**b**). Hold it up and say: 'The detectives have found the card!'

PERFORMER'S MISTAKE

This is a simple key card trick with a twist.

EFFECT

The performer appears to make a mistake, but just as the spectators are about to enjoy a laugh at the performer's expense, the tables are turned.

EQUIPMENT

An ordinary pack of playing cards.

PREPARATION

The trick uses the glimpse (*see page 22*) and false overhand shuffle (*see page 10*) techniques.

PERFORMING

● Begin by squaring the pack and glimpsing the bottom card. This is the key card (**a**).

● Shuffle the pack using a false overhand shuffle which keeps the bottom card in place.

● Give the pack face down to one spectator and ask her to cut the pack into three piles (**1**). Keep track of which pile contains the key card (**a**).

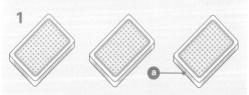

1

● Ask the spectator to look at and remember the top card of any pile, show it to the audience, and replace it on any pile.

● Your job is to ensure that the key card goes on top of the spectator's card. If she puts her chosen card (**b**) back on the pile that contains the key card, tell her to cut the pile (**2**). This puts your key card (**a**) on her card (**b**). Then ask her to put this pile on either of the other piles, and put the third pile on top.

2

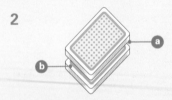

● If she puts her card on one of the other piles, point to the pile containing the key card and say: 'Put this pile on your card, and the last pile on both.' Again, your key card is on the chosen card.

● Ask the spectator to cut the pack twice; the chances of separating the key card from the spectator's are small.

● Now take the pack and deal the cards one at a time, face up, in a column of overlapping cards.

● As you deal, continue talking: 'Don't say anything. Let me find the card. I'll tell you when I see it.'

● When you get to the key card (**a**), deal the next card – the chosen one (**b**) – and keep going (**3**). Deal out four or five more cards.

● By this time, the audience will think you have missed the card. Prepare to deal out the next card and say: 'The next card I will turn over will be the chosen card. Anyone care to take a bet?' You should get some takers.

● Now, instead of turning over the next card as the audience is expecting, reach out to the column and flip over the chosen card (**b**). It is time to call in your bet.

There are many ways of inconspicuously marking a card to identify it as a key card. This is the first of two examples. Several tricks using marked cards appear later.

IMPOSSIBLE LOCATION

This highly effective trick uses a card with a bent corner as a temporarily marked key.

EFFECT
A spectator removes a card from the pack, remembers it, and returns it anywhere in the pack. The performer then takes the pack and hands it back to the spectator to shuffle. Afterwards, the performer cuts the pack and reveals the chosen card.

EQUIPMENT
A new or nearly new pack of playing cards.

PREPARATION
Practise the moves – particularly bending and unbending the corner of the card – and accompanying patter so that you can do it flawlessly every time.

PERFORMING
● Hand the pack to a spectator and ask him to shuffle it.

● Take back the pack, fan the cards with faces down and ask a spectator to remove a card, look at it and remember it.

● Close up the pack and ask the spectator to return the card to any location within the pack. As he does so,

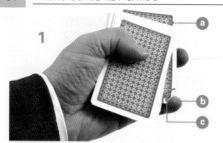

hold the pack tightly so that it is difficult to insert the card all the way.

● With a twist of your wrist, turn the pack (**1**) so that the chosen card (**a**) protrudes slightly toward you.

● Say 'Thank you' and confirm that the spectator has freely chosen where to replace the card. As you talk, use a hidden finger (**b**) to bend over one corner (**c**) of the protruding card.

● Now square up the pack and hand it back to the spectator to shuffle.

● Take back the pack. If you have bent the card correctly, it will form a slight break in the pack. Cut the cards at the break and locate the chosen card (you can even do this behind your back).

● As you remove the chosen card from the pack, run your fingers over the corner to straighten out the bend. The audience will now have no clue as to how you carried out the trick.

THE DENTED CARD

This sophisticated trick uses a dented card as the temporarily marked key.

EFFECT

The trick produces two effects. The performer is able to guess how many cards a spectator keeps in her pocket, and then correctly predicts one card she has chosen.

EQUIPMENT

A new or nearly new pack of playing cards and a sharp fingernail.

PREPARATION

Practise denting cards with your fingernail. When practising, mark the sides, not the top and bottom, of the cards.

PERFORMING

1

- Allow the spectator to remove any 12 cards from the pack. Ask her to shuffle these.

- As she is shuffling, take the rest of the deck (1) and nick the top edge of the top card with your fingernail. Turn the deck around and nick the bottom edge of the top card in the same way.

● Place the pack on the table. Your key card is on top.

● Ask the spectator to place some of the 12 cards in her pocket.

● Ask her to shuffle the cards remaining in her hand and look at and remember the bottom card. Then ask her to place the cards on top of the rest of the pack. Her chosen card is now on top of the key card.

● Hand the pack to her and ask her to deal face down a row of six overlapping cards (**2**).

● Ask her to deal face down a second row of six cards below the first.

● Look for the key card (**a**). This card is number one. Now count the cards from this one to the card at the far right of the second row. This number is the number of cards in her pocket.

Note: *If the key card is in the first row, the number will be greater than six; if it is in the second row, the number will be six or less.*

● Now tell the spectator how many cards she has in her pocket and get her to take them out and confirm this.

● Then, ask her to put a finger on one of the cards in the second row. There is a chance it is the card she originally chose (**b**) – the one just before the key card – in which case the trick is over. Ask her to turn over the card, and everyone will be amazed.

● If she places her finger on another card, scoop up all the other cards, making sure her original chosen card (**b**) is on the bottom. Glimpse this card as you add the pile to the rest of the pack.

● Now ask the spectator to turn over her card. Say: 'Ah, lovely' and pretend to go through a complicated calculation. Finally, identify the original chosen card.

2 1st row

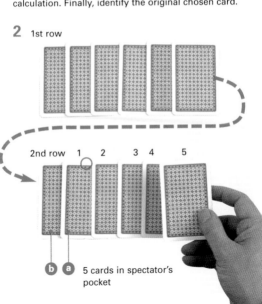

2nd row   1   2   3   4   5

b **a**   5 cards in spectator's pocket

2. Mathematical card tricks

Most of these tricks are easy to perform. They depend on the mathematical arrangement of cards rather than on card-handling skills. Try them as a simple and effective change from your normal repertoire.

ROWS AND COLUMNS

This trick is best used on a young audience. Don't use it more than once, or a spectator might catch on to how the trick works.

EFFECT
A spectator chooses a card from the pile. The card is returned to the pile. The performer spreads the cards face up in rows of six, then again but in a new arrangement. Each time, the performer asks the spectator which row contains the selected card. The performer can then find the chosen card.

EQUIPMENT
An ordinary pack of playing cards.

PREPARATION
Practise laying out the cards quickly and neatly into a tight arrangement of rows and columns.

PERFORMING

● Count out 36 cards from the pack. Shuffle this pile using an overhand shuffle.

● Ask a spectator to choose a card from the pile, put the card back, and then shuffle the pile.

1

● Take the pile and lay the cards face up in six rows of six cards each (**1**), proceeding from left to right in a row, and then starting on the next row underneath. The cards must be arranged precisely as shown, so that the cards in each row are nearly touching one another but there is a space between one row and the next. Thus the rows will be noticeable, but the columns will not.

● Ask the spectator to point out which row contains the chosen card (for example, row 3).

● Now pick up the cards in the same order in which

you put them down. Make sure you remember in which row (from the top) the chosen card is found.

2

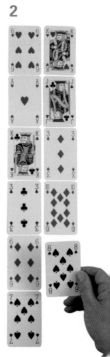

● Arrange the cards in six rows again, but lay them out as columns (2). Instead of proceeding from one row to the next, proceed from one column to the next. When you finish one column, start the next one to the right. Just as before, let the cards in the same row touch each other, but leave spaces between one row and the next.

● Once again (3), ask the spectator which row contains the chosen card (for example, row 4). At this point, you can name the card. How? If the spectator said the card was in row 3 first time round, and in row 4 second time round, then the card is located in the third column of the fourth row (a). Because of the way you have arranged the cards, rows the first time round become columns the second time round. Where the column and row intersect is where the chosen card is found.

3

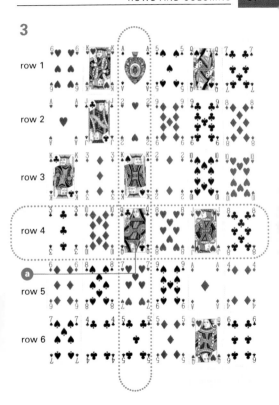

row 1

row 2

row 3

row 4

a

row 5

row 6

THREE COLUMNS

This trick is a foolproof one.

EFFECT

A spectator chooses a card and returns it to the pile. The performer spreads the cards face up in three columns of seven, three separate times. Each time, the performer asks the spectator which row contains the selected card. The performer is then able to pick out the card, which is always the middle card of the final arrangement.

EQUIPMENT

An ordinary pack of playing cards.

PREPARATION

Practise laying out the cards in three columns three times in a row, so as to consistently find the chosen card as the centre one.

PERFORMING

● Count out 21 cards from the pack. Shuffle this pile using an overhand shuffle (*see page 8*).

● Ask a spectator to first choose a card from the pile, then put the card back and shuffle the pile.

● Take the pile, and openly lay the cards face up in three columns of seven cards, proceeding from top to bottom and from left to right (1).

● Ask the spectator which column contains his selected card. Now pick up the cards in each column from top to bottom (2), starting with the first column and continuing with the column which contains the

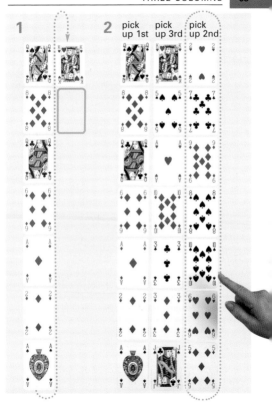

1

2 pick   pick   pick
   up 1st   up 3rd   up 2nd

chosen card – for example, the third column. Then pick up the final column. The column containing the chosen card is now sandwiched between the other two columns.

● Arrange the cards again in three columns but this time lay them out in rows. Place the first card in the first column, the second card in the second column, the third card in the third column, the fourth card in the first column and so on (3).

● Again, ask the spectator which column contains the selected card. Pick the cards up in columns, with the column containing the selected card in the middle.

● Arrange the cards again in three columns, laying them out in rows as you did the last time.

● Again, ask the spectator which column contains the chosen card. For the final time pick up the cards, as before in columns, with the chosen column in the middle.

● To finish, deal out the cards face up either in a single pile or in columns (4). In a pile, the chosen card will be the 11th card you deal out. In columns, the chosen card will be in the middle (a) – also the 11th card.

● How the trick works is as follows: The first time the spectator points out the column that contains the chosen card, you know the card is one of seven cards. When you lay the cards out a second time, you spread these seven cards out among three columns, so that each column has only two or three of them. When you lay the cards out a third time, you spread these two or three cards out so that each column contains only one of them, and always in the middle of the column. By putting the chosen column in the middle the last time you pick up the cards, you automatically make the chosen card the middle card – the 11th.

TEN IN A LINE

This trick is best used on a young audience. Providing the order of cards is not disturbed, the trick can be repeated successfully several times in a row, to the increasing bewilderment of the audience.

EFFECT

Ten cards lie face down on the table. The performer turns away from the cards and asks the audience to move up to nine cards, one at a time, from the left end of the line to the right end. The performer turns back to face the

PERFORMING

● Lay the cards face down in a row so that they are in order, from A to 10, going from left to right.

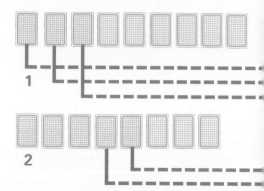

audience and turns over one of the cards in the line. The number on the card shows how many cards have been moved.

Equipment
Ten cards of mixed suits numbered from A to 10.

Preparation
Practise the trick several times with the cards face up to see how it works. Before performing the trick, prepare the ten cards so that they are in order, from A to 10.

● Tell the audience that, while your back is turned, they should move some cards from the left end of the row to the right end of the row, one card at a time. They may move up to nine cards, and you will guess

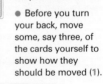

how many cards they moved.

● Before you turn your back, move some, say three, of the cards yourself to show how they should be moved (**1**).

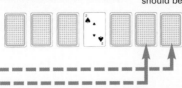

● Now, turn your back and let the audience move the cards.

● Turn back to face the audience. If in your initial demonstration you moved three cards, count three cards from the right-hand end of the row, and turn over the fourth card. The number of the card will tell you how many cards were moved. If, for example, the audience moved two cards (2, see previous page), the number on the card you turn over will be a 2.

● You can repeat this method several times, but each time you must add the moved number of cards to the previous score, and this will tell you which card to turn over. In our example, if you do the trick a second time, you need to add the three you moved to the two moved by the audience. This gives you five, the number of cards to count from the right-hand end of the row. Turning over the sixth card will tell you how many cards the audience moved the second time round.

● You can repeat the trick several times, but you have to keep a running score in your head of the total number of cards moved. Whenever the total reaches ten or more, subtract ten and use only the remainder.

Note: *If your audience tries to fool you by not moving any cards at all, you will find this out. When you turn over the card it will be a 10.*

TIME WILL TELL

This trick uses cards displayed as the hours on a clock face as a way of finding a chosen card.

EFFECT

A spectator is given a pile of cards and asked to pocket several and shuffle the rest. She memorises the bottom card and then returns the pile to the top of the pack. The performer then deals out 12 cards in a circle to form the hours on a clock face, and asks the spectator to count the cards in her pocket. That number gives the hour on the clock face where her chosen card will be.

EQUIPMENT

An ordinary pack of playing cards.

PREPARATION

Practise spreading cards between your hands so that you can quickly and easily count out 13 cards without your audience noticing.

PERFORMING

● Ask a spectator to shuffle the deck.

● Take the pack and casually spread the cards between your fingers. As you do so, silently count off 13 cards and hand them to a spectator saying, 'Here, take these.'

● Place the remainder of the pack face down on the table.

● Turn your back to the audience and explain to the spectator with the cards: 'While my back is turned, put some of your cards in your pocket. Shuffle the remainder. Now look at the bottom card and memorise it. Put those cards back on the deck on the table.'

● When the spectator has done this, turn back round. Pick up the deck and explain: 'I will deal out the cards to represent a clock face.'

● Begin to deal out 12 cards in an anticlockwise direction (1). The first card is placed at the 12 o'clock position, the next card at 11, and so on, until you have dealt a circle of cards on the table. Place the rest of the pack below the 12 o'clock card.

● Explain to the audience which card position represents each hour on the clock face.

● Ask the spectator to remove the cards she placed in her pocket earlier. Ask her: 'How many cards do you have?' For this example, let us assume she has six cards.

● Explain: 'You have six cards. Please look at the clock and point to the card that lies in the six o'clock position.'

● Ask: 'What was the name of the card you memorised?' When she names the card, ask her to turn over the card she is pointing to. It will be her card.

Note: *The trick works because the number of cards the spectator returned to the deck is always equal to 13 minus the number of cards she pocketed. If she* *pockets five, there are eight of her cards on top of the deck, and the eighth card is the one she memorised. Starting at 12 o'clock and moving anticlockwise, the memorised card will always be found at the hour indicated by the number of cards in the spectator's pocket.*

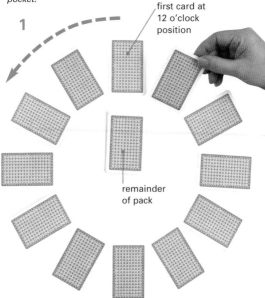

first card at 12 o'clock position

1

remainder of pack

THE NINTH CARD

This trick relies on a simple mathematical principle. Numbers 10 to 19 have a special property; when the two digits of each of these numbers are added together, and this total is subtracted from the original number, then the result will always be nine.

EFFECT
A spectator is asked to choose a number from 10 to 19, and is then asked to deal cards based on simple calculations using this number. Once completed, the performer will always be able to predict the spectator's last card.

EQUIPMENT
An ordinary pack of playing cards.

PREPARATION
The trick is straightforward. Practise quickly glimpsing the ninth card of the pack.

PERFORMING
● Shuffle the pack and then glance through it as if you are checking it for jokers. As you do so, glimpse and remember the ninth card from the top (1). (Remember that because the cards are face up, the top of the deck becomes the bottom.)

● Set the deck face down on the table in front of a spectator.

● Ask the spectator to choose a number from 10 to 19.

● Now ask him: 'Do you have that number? Good.'

Hand him the pack and say: 'Now please deal that many cards face down onto the table.'

9th card from top

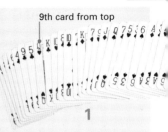

● Ask him to pick up the cards he now has on the table. Say: 'In your head, please total the digits of your original number to arrive at a single digit. For example, if you chose 13 you would add the 1 and the 3 together, giving you 4. Have you got that?' You may have to repeat your explanation.

● Say: 'You now have the new number. Deal that many cards back onto the deck from the pile in your hand.'

● When he has done this, say: 'Please look at the top card of the pile you now hold. This card was arrived at strictly by chance. Remember it.' Providing he has done his calculations correctly, the spectator will now be looking at the card that was originally the ninth card in the deck – the one you glimpsed and remembered.

● Ask the spectator to bury the card in the middle of the pack, re-form the deck and shuffle it.

● Spread the cards face up, and then run your finger along the cards as though sensing for the right card, until you stop and pick the chosen card.

THE PIANO TRICK

This is an old but reliable trick. It dates back to about 1900 and gets its name from the position of the spectator's hands – similar to that when playing the piano. Don't do the trick more than once, or someone might catch on to how it works.

Effect
The performer apparently makes a card move from one pile to another.

Equipment
Fifteen cards from an ordinary playing pack.

Preparation
Slick presentation is needed for this trick to be successful. Practise doing the moves quickly with the right accompanying patter.

Performing
● Ask to look at the hands of your spectators, and after doing so, pick out one person to be your assistant, saying: 'You have nice hands. Help me do the piano trick. Please put your hands on the table as though you were sitting at the piano keys. Let me take some cards and set them between your fingers.'

● Insert two cards, as shown (1), between adjacent fingers and between finger and thumb. Do this for both hands, starting with the spectator's right hand. When you get to the final position, between the third and fourth fingers of the left hand, place only a single card.

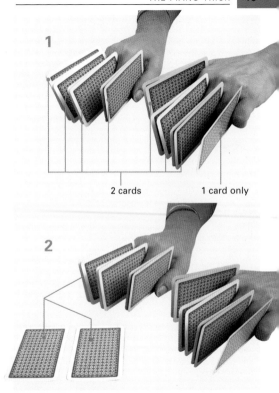

1

2 cards   1 card only

2

● Explain what you have done: 'We have placed two cards, an even number, between each of your fingers, and a single odd card here.' Show the position of the last card.

● Now remove the first two cards from between the fingers, and lay them side by side on the table (2, see previous page).

● Do the same with the next two cards, placing one card in each pile. Repeat this with all the cards, forming two equal piles, until you are left with the single remaining card.

● Ask the audience: 'On which pile shall I put the remaining card?' Add it to whichever pile is chosen.

● Continue: 'Now watch closely. I'm going to move the odd card.' Pick up the pile containing the extra card and, with a grand gesture, click the fingers of your other hand.

● Now deal out the cards in pairs and point out that the 'odd card' has disappeared.

● Pick up the other pile and deal out the cards in pairs. You will have a single card left over. Exclaim: 'Ah, here it is!'

Note: *The trick works because each pile contains seven cards. Adding the extra card to one pile makes it eight, an even number. The spectators don't catch on to this because you have misdirected them.*

YOUR DEAL

EFFECT

The spectator cuts the pack and chooses and replaces a card. By dealing the cards into piles, discarding some, the spectator miraculously holds the chosen card.

EQUIPMENT

An ordinary pack of playing cards in fairly new condition.

PREPARATION

Practise your patter so that you can quickly and clearly give instructions to a spectator. Check that you can cut the pack reliably into two equal or near equal halves.

PERFORMING

● Ask a spectator to shuffle the pack and then get her to 'cut the pack exactly in half'. This may be difficult to do, so after the cut has been made, try to even up the two piles by moving a few cards from the higher pile to the lower one. For the trick to work, the cut must be within four cards of the centre.

● Now ask her: 'Take a card from anywhere in one of the piles. Please remember the card and place it on top of its pile. Now cover it with the other pile so that it is lost in the middle of the deck.'

● Point to the table top and say: 'Deal the top four cards face down in a row here. Keep dealing the cards in this way until you have four heaps'.

● After she has dealt the cards, turn over and spread out each pile so that the cards can been seen.

● Get her to indicate which pile contains the chosen card. Turn that pile face down and discard all the other piles (1). This remaining pile should now contain 13 cards.

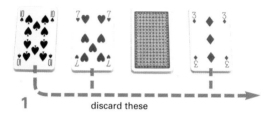

1   discard these

● Ask the spectator to deal this pile into four new piles.

● When this is done, the last card dealt should be on the first pile. Explain: 'This pile isn't even so we'll discard it.'

● That will leave three piles, each containing three cards. In fact, the middle card of the middle pile will be the chosen one.

● Ask the spectator to discard the top and bottom card of each pile. Three single cards now remain on the table.

● Pick up the three cards from left to right and hand them to the spectator. Get her to discard the top and bottom card and ask her to state her chosen card. The card remaining in her hand is the one she originally chose.

DUCK ONE, DROP TWO

This trick provides an effective change of pace in a routine. It is very easy to learn. Perform it just once, and then move on to the next trick.

EFFECT
The performer appears to mix up the order of cards according to the spectator's instructions. The cards, however, always stay in the same order.

EQUIPMENT
An ordinary pack of playing cards.

PREPARATION
Try the trick out once for yourself to see how it works.

PERFORMING

1

● Openly remove from the pack (1) ten cards of one suit, A to 10.

● Arrange them face down in a pile in sequence, with the A on top and the 10 at the bottom.

● Explain to a spectator: 'This is a simple demonstration. I will deal the cards onto the table, one at a time. As I lift each card tell me whether to deal or duck the card. Each time I duck a card I will drop it on the table with the next card. I'll show you how it works. Are you ready? Here goes.'

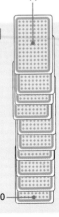

A

10

● Start to deal the cards, one at a time (2).

● When you are told to 'duck', take the card you would have dealt and slip it directly under the very next top card. Lift both of them off the deck and drop them together onto the cards on the table (3).

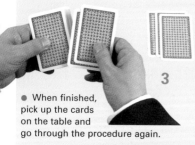

● Continue to deal or 'duck one, drop two' as the spectator requests.

● When finished, pick up the cards on the table and go through the procedure again.

● When you have done this twice, ask 'Shall we do it once more, or are you happy that they're all mixed up?' Whatever the reply, announce: 'Well, let's see.'

● Turn all the cards face up. They will still be in their original order. Act surprised and say: 'Well I never!'

A PROCESS OF ELIMINATION

EFFECT
The performer spreads the cards and a spectator takes one and returns it to the pack. The performer then sorts the cards into two piles – one face up, the other face down. The spectator is asked to say when the card appears in the face-up pile. It never does. The performer repeats the procedure over and over again until left with one card – the spectator's card.

EQUIPMENT
An ordinary pack of playing cards.

PREPARATION
Practise spreading the cards with ease and precision so that you can reliably count out 21 cards in one hand.

PERFORMING
● Spread the deck of cards face down between your hands so that your spectator can choose a card (1).

1

21 cards

2 (a)

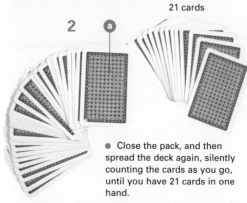

● Close the pack, and then spread the deck again, silently counting the cards as you go, until you have 21 cards in one hand.

● Ask the spectator to place his card (**a**) on top of the pile in your other hand (**2**), and then replace the pile of 21 cards on top. The selected card is now 22nd from the top.

● Now explain: 'I'll deal some cards face up and some face down. Watch the face-up group. Look for your card, but don't tell me when I pass it.'

● Start to deal the cards (**3**). The first card is placed face up in front of your spectator; the next card face down near you; the third card face up near him; the fourth card face down near you. Continue in this way until you have two piles of cards, one face up and one face down.

card from top of the pile

next card down

● When all the cards have been dealt, ask the spectator whether he has seen his card. The answer should be 'no.'

● Push the face-up pile of cards to one side, and pick up the face-down pile of cards. Deal these cards as before: first face up, second face down, and so on.

● When you have finished dealing, again ask your spectator whether he has seen his card. He should still answer 'no.'

● Keep repeating this procedure until you have been through the entire pack without him seeing his card. The very last face-down card in your hand will be his card.

A MAGIC SEQUENCE

This is a simple novelty trick which can be performed only once using a prearranged pack.

EFFECT

The performer quickly shows 13 cards to an audience – the cards appear to be out of sequence. The performer then deals alternate cards face up on the table and places every other card at the bottom of the pack. Soon the entire sequence, from A to K, is assembled on the table as if by magic.

EQUIPMENT

An ordinary pack of playing cards.

PREPARATION

Arrange the following cards, of mixed suit, in this order at the top of the face-down pack: a 10 on top, then a 6, K, 5, 9, 4, J, 3, 8, 2, Q, A and finally a 7. The sequence of the rest of the pack does not matter.

PERFORMING

● Pick up the pack and deal the top 13 cards face down in a pile on the table. Put the rest of the pack aside.

● Pick up the pile of 13 cards and briefly fan them face out towards the audience – do this quickly, so that the spectators have just enough time to see that the cards are not in a simple sequence (1). Explain: 'You can see that the cards are not in order. But look what happens . . .'

1

● Now keep the cards face down in one hand and deal them out in the following manner: take the top card and place it face down underneath the pile, then deal the next card face up on the table (**2**). Continue alternating the cards in this way until you have dealt out all the cards.

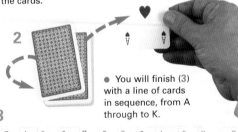

2

● You will finish (**3**) with a line of cards in sequence, from A through to K.

3

3. Tricks using arranged stacks of cards

Knowing the exact position of some or all of the cards in a pack enables you to perform some startling tricks. To use a stacked deck – one in which the cards are arranged in a particular order – you need a system which is easy to remember but difficult for onlookers to spot.

SI STEBBINS

Si Stebbins was an American vaudeville performer who developed this system and kept it a secret for 40 years.

EFFECT
The Si Stebbins system is used to perform a whole range of tricks. In its simplest form, as described here, a spectator can pick any card from the pack. With a cut of the pack, the performer immediately names the chosen card. Various ways of revealing the card make the performance more entertaining.

EQUIPMENT
An ordinary pack of playing cards.

PREPARATION
The trick requires use of the glimpse (*see page 22*). The cards need to be arranged beforehand in a specific sequence:

● Each card in the sequence has a value of three more than the preceding card. For example, if the first card in

the pack is a 3, the second is a 6, and the third is a 9.
Note: *The J has a value of 11, the Q 12 and the K 13. The A is always 1.*

● The order of suits is clubs, hearts, spades, diamonds. For example, if the first card is the 3 of clubs, the second is the 6 of hearts, the third is the 9 of spades and the fourth is the Q of diamonds. The order is remembered using the mnemonic CHaSeD.

● To arrange the pack, divide it first into four stacks of 13 cards (3 to K) ordered in the sequence described above. The stacks are:

3–C	3–H	3–S	3–D
6–H	6–S	6–D	6–C
9–S	9–D	9–C	9–H
Q–D	Q–C	Q–H	Q–S
2–C	2–H	2–S	2–D
5–H	5–S	5–D	5–C
8–S	8–D	8–C	8–H
J–D	J–C	J–H	J–S
A–C	A–H	A–S	A–D
4–H	4–S	4–D	4–C
7–S	7–D	7–C	7–H
10–D	10–C	10–H	10–S
K–C	K–H	K–S	K–D

● Then put the stacks together, one on top of the other left to right, to form the pack.

Note: *Cutting the pack does not alter the sequence of cards; it simply changes the starting point.*

PERFORMING

● Fan the cards face down towards a spectator (1) and ask her to remove a card of her choice.

● Cut the pack at the point where she removed the card.

● Glance at the bottom card, which was above the spectator's chosen card. Simply add three to the value of the bottom card and determine which suit follows that of the bottom card. Now you can name the spectator's chosen card. For example, if the bottom card is the 5 of diamonds, the chosen card is the 8 of clubs.

Note: *If you intend to repeat the trick, make sure that you return the spectator's card to the top of the pack so the sequence is unbroken. Use a riffle shuffle (see page 13) when you wish to break up the stacked arrangement of the cards.*

THE JOKER KNOWS

This trick uses an entertaining method of revealing the spectator's card.

EFFECT
The spectator chooses a card and puts it in her pocket without looking at it. The performer uses a joker to help predict the chosen card.

EQUIPMENT
An ordinary pack of playing cards, plus a single joker.

PREPARATION
The pack needs to be arranged according to the Si Stebbins system (*see page 86*), with a joker placed at random. It requires the use of the glimpse technique (*see page 22*).

PERFORMING
● Fan the cards face up so you and the audience can see them.

● Openly remove the joker and place it face down on the table.

● Give the deck a few cuts and then spread the cards face down and ask the spectator to take one and put it in her pocket without looking at it.

● Cut the deck at the point where the card was removed, and glimpse the bottom card as you complete the cut.

● The bottom card will tell you the name of the spectator's chosen card. For example, if the 3 of diamonds is the bottom card, the top card is the 6 of clubs.

● Now pick up the joker and put it to your ear (1) as though you are listening for something. To make the trick more dramatic pretend to get the information in stages. Say, for example: 'It's a black card. It's a 6. Ah, it's the 6 of clubs.'

● Finish with: 'Jokers are pretty useful sometimes!'

COUNTING THE CARDS

You need to be good at mental arithmetic to perform this trick.

EFFECT
The performer riffles through the pack, and the observer is invited to say 'stop' at any time. The deck is broken at that point, and the spectator is handed the larger pile. Within seconds – without counting the cards – the performer tells the spectator how many cards she holds.

EQUIPMENT
An ordinary pack of playing cards.

PREPARATION
The pack needs to be arranged using the Si Stebbins system *(see page 86)*. The trick uses the glimpse technique *(see page 22)*.

PERFORMING
● Hold the pack vertically with one hand, facing away from you, and with the other hand riffle through the pack (1).

● Ask a spectator to call 'stop' at any time.

● When the spectator calls 'stop', break the deck at that point and hand the spectator the pile with the

2

largest number of cards. As you do this, make a show of weighing both piles face up in your hands (2). This gives you time to glimpse her bottom card and start to do a mental calculation.

● Note the bottom card of her pile (for example, the 5 of hearts) and the bottom card of your pile (for example, the J of clubs). Then give the spectator her pile.

● To work out the number of cards you and she are holding, perform the following mental calculations.

● First, you must determine the value of the nearest card in your pile that is of the same suit as the spectator's bottom card (in this case, hearts).

Note: *If the spectator's bottom card is of the same suit as your bottom card, there is no need to calculate this.*

Using the mnemonic CHaSeD, work backwards from C (clubs) to H (hearts) to calculate how far away the

3

CHaSeDCHaSeD

nearest heart is. In this case
(3), it is three cards away.

Take the number of cards (in
this case 3) and multiply it
by 3 (the increase in value
from one card to the next in
the system). Subtract this
number from the value of
your bottom card.

$$3 \times 3 = 9$$

$$11 - 9 = 2$$

You now know that the nearest card of the same suit
is the 2 of hearts. Knowing this, you can do the rest of
the calculations.

Of the two same-suit cards,
subtract the lower number
from the higher one.

$$5 - 2 = 3$$

Then multiply this number
by 4.

$$3 \times 4 = 12$$

If the spectator's bottom card is of the same suit as
your bottom card, then this (in this case, 12) is the
number of cards in one pile. If the bottom cards are of
different suits, do the next calculation.

Add on the number of cards between your bottom card and the nearest card in your pile which is of the same suit as the spectator's bottom card.

12 + 3 = 15

This gives you the number of cards in *one* pile.

Subtract this number from 52 to give the number of cards in the other hand.

52 − 15 = 37

Announce the number of cards the spectator is holding. Have her confirm your 'guess' by counting her pile of cards as she deals them face down.

● The above calculation will work in all cases but one. If the spectator's bottom card has the same value as yours, then you know that the two cards are multiples of 13 away from one another – in other words, your pile (the smaller one) has either 13 or 26 cards. Unless your piles appear to be equal (and both thus have 26 cards), her pile must have 39 cards (52 − 13 = 39).

Note: *You can repeat the trick, but the spectator's stack must be put back in the right place to maintain the order of cards.*

MULTIPLE IDENTIFICATION

This is an effective trick for use with three or more
spectators. It relies on spotting disruptions in the sequence
of cards.

EFFECT
Three spectators each choose a card from different parts of
the pack. The cards are then pushed back into the pack at
three different locations. The performer cuts the pack
several times and picks out the three cards.

EQUIPMENT
An ordinary pack of playing cards.

PREPARATION
The pack needs to be arranged according to the Si Stebbins
system (*see page 86*).

PERFORMING
- Fan the cards face down (**1**) and ask three spectators
  each to remove one card from different
  parts of the pack.

1

● Ask the spectators to memorise their selected cards and then return them to the pack but at a different location.

● Cut the cards a few times and then fan them out so only you can see their faces.

● In the Si Stebbins system, each card should have a value three higher than the card to its left. If it does not, then you know a card has been added or removed from that position.

● You can now pick (**2**) out the three selected cards (**a**). They will be the ones out of sequence – but remember, their original locations will leave 'gaps' (**b**) in the sequence.

● Place the three selected cards face down on the table.

● Ask the spectators to name their cards. Turn the cards over and take your bow.

Note: *You will have to put the cards back in their original locations if you want to use the stacked sequence in further tricks.*

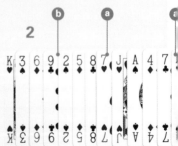

THE THREE PILES

This trick uses a stacked deck to identify one selected card. The performer uses this information to stay one step ahead of the audience and so identify two other cards.

EFFECT
The performer cuts the pack several times, and then divides the pack into three piles and correctly identifies the top cards of all three piles.

EQUIPMENT
An ordinary pack of playing cards.

PREPARATION
The pack needs to be arranged according to the Si Stebbins system (*see page 86*). You will need to practise the false overhand shuffle (*see page 10*) and glimpse technique (*see page 22*), and you will probably need to practise this trick several times to get the order of moves right.

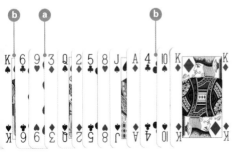

PERFORMING

● Do a false shuffle, which keeps all the cards in the same order.

● Cut the cards, re-form the pack and then square the cards, glimpsing the bottom card as you do so.

● From the value and suit of the bottom card, calculate the value and suit of the top card, the next card in the stacked sequence. For example, under Si Stebbins, if the bottom card is the 2 of spades, the top card is the 5 of diamonds.

● Now divide the pack into three piles (or get a spectator to do it for you). Keep your eye on the final position of the top pile. This is the pile whose top card you know. In the steps that follow, you will come to this pile last.

● Tap your finger on one of the other piles (1) and say confidently: 'This is the 5 of diamonds'.

● Pick up the top card from that pile (**c**) and hold it facing you.

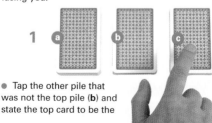

● Tap the other pile that was not the top pile (**b**) and state the top card to be the one you are actually holding. So, if you picked up the Q of clubs from the first pile, you tap the second pile and say: 'This is the Q of clubs.'

● Once again remove the top card and hold it facing you to the right of the first card.

● Now tap the third pile (**a**), which you know to be the top pile, and state the top card to be the one you picked from the second pile. For example, if you picked up the J of spades, call this as the top card of the third pile. (You know this card actually to be the 5 of diamonds.)

● Remove the top card from the third pile and place it to the left of the two cards in your hand.

● Place the three cards face up on the table and show that you have correctly identified them (**2**).

Note: *If you are careful, you can place the cards back on their original piles and retain the stacked sequence to perform further tricks. Alternatively, riffle shuffle the pack (see page 13) to break up the sequence.*

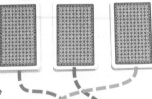

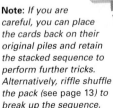

LISTEN TO THE QUEEN

This trick is a particularly effective last trick before breaking up a stacked deck.

EFFECT

The spectator cuts the cards three times and then takes the top card. He then takes out a Q from a face-up fan of cards and hands it to the performer, who 'listens' to the Q and correctly predicts the spectator's card.

EQUIPMENT

An ordinary pack of playing cards.

PREPARATION

The pack needs to be arranged according to the Si Stebbins system (*see page 86*). This trick requires the use of the glimpse technique (*see page 22*).

PERFORMING

● Spread the deck face up on the table and announce: 'As you can see, the deck is not stacked in any way.' Scoop the cards up before the spectators realise this is not the case.

● Hand the deck to a spectator and ask him to cut the pack once, and then once again. Then add: 'Just to be sure, cut it a third time.'

● Instruct the spectator to take the top card and, without looking at it, to place it face down on the table.

● Ask for the pack, and then fan the cards face up

1

and ask the spectator to choose a Q (**1**). As you do this, glimpse the bottom card. This will be the card that is directly before the chosen card in the arranged sequence. You can now identify the chosen card. For example, the 2 of clubs on the bottom of the pack will mean the spectator's card is the 5 of hearts.

● Place the pack face down and take the Q from the spectator.

● Put the Q to your ear and pretend to be listening for information.

● Say to the spectator: 'When you looked for the Q could you tell which card was missing? No? Neither could I. But the Q is very helpful. She tells me the card you took is the [in this case, the 5 of hearts].'

● Ask the spectator to turn over the card and confirm that the Q is correct.

● Re-form the pack and riffle shuffle the cards (*see page 13*) to break up the sequence.

A DREAM COME TRUE

This trick is particularly useful in the company of poker players and is an effective trick to break up a stacked deck. It requires three spectators.

EFFECT

The performer spreads the cards face up to show the spectators, cuts the pack and then deals out four hands face down, as though playing poker. When the cards are turned over, all hands show a straight flush (five cards of the same suit in number order – for example, 4, 5, 6, 7, 8). The last hand – the performer's – is a royal flush (10, J, Q, K, A) and beats all the others!

EQUIPMENT

An ordinary pack of playing cards.

PREPARATION

The pack needs to be arranged according to the Si Stebbins system (*see page 86*).

PERFORMING

● Spread the deck face up on the table. Announce: 'As you can see, the deck is not stacked in any way.' Scoop the cards up before the spectators realise this is not the case.

● As you scoop up the cards, look for a 2 and then cut the deck at that point, so the 2 is on the bottom.

● Say: 'Let's play some poker, and I'll show you a dream come true.'

● Deal out the cards face down as you would for four hands in a game of five-card poker – that is, one card to each player, and going round five times so that each player ends up with five cards. As the dealer, you get the fourth hand.

● Start with the first hand (1) and turn it over saying: 'Let's see what you got.' It will be a 5-high straight flush. Say: 'Not bad.'

● Repeat with the second (2) and third (3) hands; they will be progressively higher straight flushes.

● Finish with your hand (4) and say: 'A royal flush. A dream come true.'

A SPECIAL ARRANGEMENT

This trick uses some stacked cards, but they are heavily disguised.

EFFECT

The performer extracts two suits of cards from the pack, seemingly at random, and gives one suit to a spectator and keeps the other. When the performer's cards are dealt, they form a straight run from A to K. When the spectator tries this, her cards are out of sequence.

EQUIPMENT

An ordinary pack of playing cards.

1

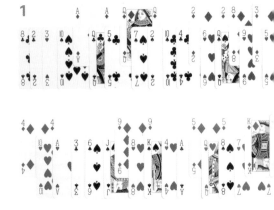

PREPARATION

Remove all the diamonds from the deck and arrange them from the top card down as follows: A, Q, 2, 8, 3, J, 4, 9, 5, K, 6, 10, 7.

Shuffle the remaining cards thoroughly.

Turn the deck face up and replace the diamonds at various points in the pack. It does not matter where you put them, but you must retain the order (1).

Put the pack to one side ready for use.

PERFORMING

● Spread the cards face up on the table.

● Begin by saying: 'Here are 52 cards. We'll need two suits.'

● Pick up the deck and say to a spectator: 'You take the hearts and I'll take the diamonds.'

● Spread out the cards again, left to right and, starting at the left, pick out the cards of each suit. When you come to a heart, drop it face up in front of the spectator.

2

When you come to a diamond, drop it face up near yourself (**2**). Make sure you keep your diamonds in the original order.

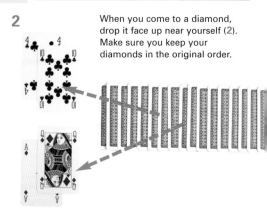

● Pick up your pile and ask the spectator to do the same. Put the remaining cards to one side.

● Say to the spectator: 'Follow me.' Then lay down your top card face up on the table – it will be an A.

● Take the next card and place it at the bottom of the pack. Make sure the spectator is doing the same.

● Deal the next one face up – it will be a 2.

● Carry on in this way, ducking one and dealing one, until you have the whole sequence before you.

● The spectator, who has been doing everything you have done, will be surprised to find that her cards are not in sequence.

THE CARD IN THE MIDDLE

This trick requires no calculations to be performed. Use it only once or your audience might catch on.

EFFECT
The performer shuffles the pack and asks the spectator to cut the pack. The performer then picks up the pack and predicts which card is in the centre (that is, which is 26th from the top). The performer then deals out the cards and shows the prediction to be correct.

EQUIPMENT
An ordinary pack of playing cards.

PREPARATION
The pack needs to be arranged according to the Si Stebbins system (*see page 86*). The trick uses the false overhand shuffle and glimpse techniques (*see page 10* and *page 22*).

Performing

● Cut the deck several times rapidly to give the appearance of shuffling the deck. In reality, you are only cutting the deck. The order remains the same.

● Explain: 'While I am shuffling the deck please call out "stop" any time you like.'

● When the spectator calls 'stop', glimpse the bottom card.

● Say: 'I'm getting better at predicting the middle card of the pack', and give your prediction. The 26th card will always be the same number as the bottom card and in the other suit of the same colour. For example, if the bottom card is the 3 of spades, the 26th card will be the 3 of clubs.

● Pass the cards to the spectator and ask him to count down to the 26th card – it will be the predicted card.

CALLING THE CARDS

This is a powerful trick using a stacked deck and involving as many spectators as you can manage – a good trick for parties. You need a good memory!

EFFECT
A spectator picks a number of cards from the pack, keeps the top card, and distributes the other cards among the spectators. The performer proceeds to identify the first spectator's card, and then all the other spectators' cards.

EQUIPMENT
An ordinary pack of playing cards.

PREPARATION
The pack needs to be arranged according to the Si Stebbins system (*see page 86*).

PERFORMING
● Fan the cards face down towards a spectator. Have him take a batch of cards from one location in the pack (you can specify the number or leave it up to the spectator: the number of cards taken should roughly correspond to the number of people in the audience or the number of cards you feel you can manage in the trick).

● As the spectator removes the cards, place your little finger at the break point in the pack. Cut the pack at this point.

● When the spectator has removed the cards, ask him to keep the cards face down, remove the top card and place it in his pocket without looking at it.

● Have the spectator shuffle his remaining cards and hand them, one at a time, to other spectators. The spectators are to look at their cards and keep them. While all this is happening, glimpse the bottom card of the pack. Knowing the stacked arrangement, you can work out which card the first spectator has. The value is three greater than the value of the bottom card, and the suit is determined using the mnemonic CHaSeD. (If the bottom card is the 5 of clubs, for example, the spectator's card is the 8 of hearts.) From this, you can identify all the cards distributed among the audience.

● At this point summarise what has happened so far: 'A number of cards have been removed from the deck, shuffled, and then distributed among you. I will now try to identify all the cards taken.'

● Name the card the first spectator has in his pocket. Get him to take it out and confirm your prediction.

● Now get the other spectators to concentrate on their cards. Pretend you are engaged in a mind–reading exercise and make a show of concentrating hard with your eyes shut. To make it more interesting, let your predictions trickle out slowly by saying, for example: 'I see a black picture card . . . Yes, the jack of spades.'

● If you look at people's reactions carefully, you may well be able to work out who is holding which card. As you predict each card, have the owner hand it back to you, and then move on to the next card. Aim to give the impression that you not only know what the cards are, but also who has which card.

ACES AND KINGS

This is a quick and simple trick using a partially stacked deck.

EFFECT
The performer shuffles the cards and then demonstrates to the spectator how he wants her to deal the cards face down into four piles. When she has done this, she discovers an A at the top of each pile. When the performer turns over each pile, a K is revealed at the bottom of each.

EQUIPMENT
An ordinary pack of playing cards.

PREPARATION
You will need to practise the false overhand shuffle (*see page 10*). Prepare the deck (**1**) by placing four As at the top of the deck followed by four Ks. The rest of the pack is in any order.

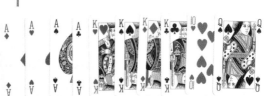

PERFORMING

● Use a false overhand shuffle which keeps the top portion of the pack in place but gives the appearance of mixing all the cards.

● Set the deck face down in front of the spectator.

● Begin by saying: 'Please cut a small number of cards from the top of the pack. I'll take them.'

● Take the small pile and say: 'What I want you to do is deal four piles onto the table.' Demonstrate this by dealing the four top cards (the As) face down onto the table in four piles.

● Now (2) place the remainder of the small pile (**a**) back on top of the pack (**b**) and nonchalantly scoop up the four As (**c**) and place them at the bottom

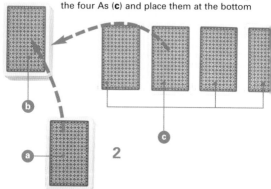

2

of the pack. All this should look relaxed as though you are simply demonstrating what the spectator has to do.

● Have the spectator deal out the four piles.

● When she has finished, ask: 'What is your favourite ace?' Whatever she replies, ask her to turn over the top card of one of the piles (). If she hits the right A first time, you will have an amazed spectator. Have her turn over the top card of all the piles and so reveal the four As.

3

● Finish with the throwaway line: 'Personally, I prefer the kings.' Reach out and turn over each pile (4) to reveal the K at the bottom of each.

4

EVEN BETTER THAN KINGS

This is another quick and simple trick using a partially stacked deck.

EFFECT
The performer shuffles the cards and gives them to a spectator and directs him to deal the cards face down into two piles. The spectator then deals each of these piles into two more piles, making four piles in all. The spectator discovers a K at the top of each pile. When he discards the Ks he then discovers an A at the top of each pile.

EQUIPMENT
An ordinary pack of playing cards.

PREPARATION
You will need to practise the false overhand shuffle (*see page 10*). Prepare the deck by placing four Ks at the top of the deck (**1**) followed by four As. The rest of the pack is in any order.

1

PERFORMING

● Use a false overhand shuffle which keeps the top portion of the pack in place but gives the appearance of mixing all the cards.

● Set the deck face down in front of the spectator and begin: 'I just want to check that something that happens when I deal will also happen when you deal. Now, just deal the pack into two face-down piles, alternating the cards.'

● Allow the spectator to deal out about half the pack and then add: 'You can stop any time you wish.'

● When he finishes (it does not matter if he deals the entire pack), take the remainder of the cards and continue: 'Now pick up one of the two piles and deal that pile into two piles. Do the same with the other pile so that we now have four piles in all.' Dealing out the piles in this way will bring the Ks back to the top with the As just below them.

● 'I think you've just dealt me my favourite cards. Turn over the top card of a pile and see what we've got.' He will now reveal a K.

● Ask: 'What about the other piles?' The spectator should now discover a K at the top of every pile.

● Have the spectator discard the Ks and say: 'Of course, we can go one better.' Close your eyes and pass your hands over the four piles. Then add: 'Let's see what we have now.' Turn over the top cards to reveal the four As.

● Finish by saying: 'Yes, it works for you too!'

4. Tricks using sleights of hand

These tricks depend on skilful sleight of hand and require good card-handling skills.

ABRACADABRA

EFFECT
A card is transformed into the spectator's chosen card.

EQUIPMENT
An ordinary pack of playing cards.

PREPARATION
You will need to practise the false overhand shuffle (*see page 10*) and the double lift (*see page 23*).

PERFORMING
● Hand the pack to a spectator and ask him to shuffle it.

● Take the pack back and fan the cards face down towards the audience.

● Ask the spectator to take a card and look at it. While you are shuffling the pack, ask the spectator to return the card to the middle of the pack as you stop momentarily.

● Discreetly insert a little finger into the pack to form a break at the point where the card was returned (1). Then use a false overhand shuffle to get the chosen card to the top of the pack.

● Turn the pack so the bottom card faces out. Ask the spectator: 'Is this your card?' He should say: 'No.'

● Do a double lift and show to the audience what looks like the top card but is really the second card. Ask: 'Is this it?' Again, he should say: 'No.'

● Hand the pack to the spectator and ask him to tap lightly on the top card and say 'Abracadabra'. Then ask him to turn it over, revealing his chosen card.

CARDS CHANGE PLACES

EFFECT
Two cards taken at random apparently change places.

EQUIPMENT
An ordinary pack of playing cards is needed.

PREPARATION
You will need to practise the double lift (*see page 23*).

PERFORMING
● Hand the pack to a spectator and ask her to shuffle it.

● Take the pack back and, while squaring the cards, separate the top two cards from the others and push them a little to the side in readiness for the double lift.

● Remark that you will use the top card, whatever it may be, to conduct an experiment. Use the double lift (**1**) and show the card to the audience; they think they are seeing the top card, but you are actually showing them the second card. For this example, it is the 3 of clubs.

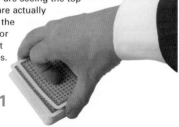

1

● Return the cards to the top of the pack and then take the top card (**a**) and place it face down on the table. The audience thinks this is the 3 of clubs; it is not – that card is still on top of the pack.

● Continue by saying: 'Let us see what the next card is', as you square the deck and get ready for another double lift. Again, take two cards as one and reveal, for example, the 8 of hearts. Say: 'Fine. That's a good contrast with our earlier card, the 3 of clubs.'

2

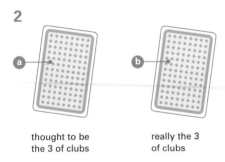

thought to be
the 3 of clubs

really the 3
of clubs

● As before, return the two cards to the top of the pack, and take the top card and place it to one side face down on the table beside the first face-down card (**2**). The spectators think this is the 8 of hearts – it is actually the 3 of clubs (**b**). The 8 of hearts remains on top of the pack.

3

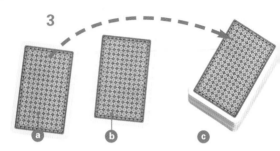

- Tell the audience: 'Remember the two cards, the 3 of clubs here [point to the first card (**a**)] and the 8 of hearts here [point to the second card (**b**)].'

- 'I'll replace the 3 back on top of the pack.' Pick up the first card (**3**), look at it, and put it on top of the pack (**c**). Don't let anyone else see the card; the audience thinks this is the 3 of clubs.

- Say: 'Now comes the remarkable bit. I'm going to make the 3 and 8 change places.' Tap the top of the pack, then pick up the deck and with a double lift show the second card from the top – the 8 of hearts.

- Ask a spectator to pick up the remaining card on the table – it will be the 3 of clubs.

- Finish by saying: 'Don't ask me to do it again. That took effort,' and continue with the next trick.

COUNTDOWN

This trick is particularly effective because the 'magic' happens in the spectator's hands, not the performer's.

EFFECT
The performer fails to find the spectator's card and hands the pack to the spectator. The spectator then follows the performer's instructions and reveals the chosen card.

EQUIPMENT
An ordinary pack of playing cards.

PREPARATION
You will need to practise the false overhand shuffle (*see page 10*).

PERFORMING
- Hand the pack to a spectator and ask him to shuffle.

- Take the pack back and fan the cards face down towards the audience.

- Ask another spectator to take a card, look at it, and return it to the middle of the pack (1) as you stop momentarily while shuffling.

● Discreetly insert a little finger into the pack to form a break at the point where the card was returned. Then use a false overhand shuffle to get the chosen card to the top of the pack.

● Ask a spectator for a number between five and 15. Count out loud and deal that number of cards into a face-down pile (the chosen card will now be on the bottom of this pile).

● When you deal out the last card, turn it over as though you are expecting this to be the chosen card. When you ask the spectator, and discover it isn't his chosen card, pretend to be disappointed.

● Turn the top card face down, scoop up the pile and place it on top of the pack.

● Hold the pack and close your eyes for a moment, as though deep in concentration and waiting for inspiration.

● Suddenly 'realise' what you have done wrong. Explain that you've been told what to do now.

● Pass the pack to the spectator and ask him to deal and count as you did before (2). This time, when the last card is turned over, it will be the correct one!

2

TWO OUT OF 52

EFFECT

Two spectators each remove a card from somewhere in the pack. They look at and return the cards. The performer shuffles the pack and then throws the cards into the air. As the cards fall to the ground the performer miraculously plucks out the two chosen cards from the falling shower of cards.

EQUIPMENT

An ordinary pack of playing cards.

PREPARATION

You will need to practise the false overhand shuffle (*see page 10*) to get two chosen cards to the top and bottom of the pack.

PERFORMING

● Hand the pack to a spectator and ask him to shuffle.

● Take back the pack, fan the cards with faces down and ask two spectators each to remove a card and remember it.

● Close up the pack, and shuffle it. Then cut the deck and ask the two spectators to return their cards – one on top of the other – in the centre of the pack where you have made the cut.

● Discreetly insert a little finger into the pack to form a break at the point where the cards were returned. Carry on shuffling and use a false overhand shuffle to get the two chosen cards to the top of the pack.

1

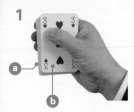

● Finally, with your last shuffle move, bring the top card to the bottom, so that the two chosen cards (**a** and **b**) are at the top and bottom of the pack.

● Explain that the next bit will be dramatic. Roll your sleeves up. This will emphasise the dramatic effect and will also prove you don't have anything 'up your sleeve'.

● Lick the thumb and fingers of your right hand. This again increases the dramatic effect, but is also needed to perform the trick.

● Hold the pack tightly between the thumb and fingers of your right hand (**1**).

● Turn your left side to the audience and throw the cards into the air. As you do this, the top and bottom cards will stay stuck to your fingers and thumb. Bring your right hand quickly to your side after throwing the pack.

● As the cards fall, plunge your right hand into the middle of the shower of cards and pretend to pull out the two cards (2).

● Show the spectators the two cards you have caught' – they are the two cards they chose!

2

THE CUT FORCE

This trick uses a simple yet powerful technique which ensures that the spectator takes a card predetermined by the performer.

EFFECT
The spectator appears to have a free choice as to which card to take. Whichever card is chosen, the performer can immediately identify it and can reveal it in a variety of ways.

EQUIPMENT
An ordinary pack of playing cards.

PREPARATION
You will need to practise the glimpse technique (*see page 22*).

PERFORMING
● Shuffle the cards and discreetly glimpse and remember the bottom card. Control the shuffle and bring this card to the top; then glimpse and remember the new bottom card. You now know the top and bottom cards of the pack.

● Place the deck on the table in front of a spectator. Say to her: 'Please cut the cards in half and place the bottom half crossways on the top half' (**1**).

● Distract the audience for a moment or two by explaining the origins of card tricks. Say, for example, 'Did you know that cards came to Europe in the

1

fourteenth century . . . probably from Egypt? We're not sure where cards were invented in the first place . . . probably India or the Middle East.'

● Then return to the pack. 'You've cut the cards and chosen where to make the cut. Lift the cards at the cut and choose either the bottom or top card.'

● Whichever card is chosen, you will know what it is. How you choose to reveal the card is up to you. One way is to ask the spectator to shuffle the pack and then slowly spread the cards face up on the table. Pretend to identify the chosen card by noticing her reaction when she uncovers it.

● Alternatively, you could pick out a bunch of cards and then, by 'noting her reactions', home in on the right card.

ONE OUT OF FIVE

This trick relies on a good memory, acting ability and dexterity.

EFFECT
The performer is able to select which one of five cards the spectator is thinking about.

EQUIPMENT
An ordinary pack of playing cards.

PREPARATION
Place any four cards in your jacket side pocket, lying horizontally with their backs facing outwards.

PERFORMING
● Ask a spectator to shuffle the pack.

● Take back the pack and spread the cards face up on the table and allow the spectator to take out any five cards.

● Take the cards and arrange them in any sequence that is easy for you to remember; for example, you can group the numbers, or work out a relationship between them. Two examples are shown (1).

For example, remember as: 24 and 89 and Q

or as: 2 x 4 = 8 (+1Q) = 9

● Now ask the spectator to think of one of the five cards. As she does this, put the five cards (**a**) in your pocket (**2**), arranged vertically and placed behind the other four cards (**b**).

2

● Casually pick up the pack, close your eyes and pretend to be concentrating hard. 'Ah, I think I have it!'

● Put your hand into your pocket and one by one take out each of the four horizontal cards, saying 'It's not this one, or this . . . .' Don't show these cards to the audience but simply place them face down on top of the pack.

● Put your hand back in your pocket and slip a finger between each of the five cards. 'There is only one card left in my pocket. It should be the one you selected. Which card did you choose?'

● When she names the card you can produce it from your pocket easily. Leave the other four cards there and put the pack in your pocket. If the audience asks to see the pack, bring it out with the other four cards on top – where they ought to be.

TURN-ABOUT

This trick has an impressive conclusion.

Effect

A spectator cuts the pack in half and takes the top half while the performer takes the bottom half. Spectator and performer each choose a card from their stack and then place it in the other's pile. The performer combines the two stacks into one, and miraculously the two chosen cards are reversed with respect to all other cards.

Equipment

An ordinary pack of playing cards.

Preparation

Prearrange the pack by memorising the bottom card and reversing it with respect to the other cards.

Performing

● Fan the cards toward the audience so that the card faces can be seen but the reversed card at the bottom is not visible.

● Instruct one spectator: 'Please cut off about half the pack.' Get him to shuffle the top pile of cards, while you take the bottom pile.

● Ask him to take one card out of the centre of his pile, look at it and memorise it. Go through the motions of doing the same with your pile, but don't bother to remember your card.

● Tell the spectator: 'I'll place my card in your half.'

As you push your card into his pile, momentarily drop your hand to your side so that your pile of cards is out of sight for a moment. Turn your pile around so your bottom card – the reversed one – is now on top.

● Take the spectator's card and push it into the middle of your pile. Make sure you put it face down. (Your pile is really face up with the exception of the top card.)

● 'Now please give me half of your pile.' Take these cards (**1**) (**a**) from the spectator, and place them face up on top of your pile (**b**).

● Take the other half of his pile (**c**) and place those face up on the bottom of your stack. Hold the three piles in your hand for a moment so that all three piles are visible. Your cards will appear to be face down, while the spectator's cards are face up.

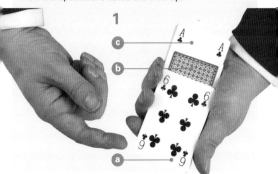

● Now push all the cards together into a single stack.

● 'I will now achieve two things with one click of my fingers. Watch closely. I will make all the cards in the pack face in the same direction but with two exceptions – your card and my card. Here we go.'

● Make a big show of clicking the fingers of one hand and as you do so turn the pack upside down, so that the top card is now face down.

● 'My card was the [give the name of the card you reversed before starting the trick]. What was yours?'

● After he has named his card, spread all the cards in a ribbon across the table (2). All will be face down, except for the two cards – your reversed card and his chosen card.

2

PICK A NUMBER

This trick is particularly effective because it combines the free choices of two spectators.

EFFECT
One spectator picks a card; another spectator picks a number. The performer then proceeds to find the chosen card at that number place in the pack.

EQUIPMENT
An ordinary pack of playing cards.

PREPARATION
This trick uses the false overhand shuffle (*see page 10*), false riffle shuffle (*see page 15*) and glide (*see page 21*).

PERFORMING
● Ask a spectator to shuffle the pack.

● Take back the pack and spread the cards in a fan face down towards the audience.

● Ask a spectator to pick a card, look at it and remember it.

● In your hand, square up the cards and ask the spectator to place the chosen card on top of the pack.

● Make a show of rolling up your sleeves to convince the audience that nothing is hidden.

● Now with a false overhand shuffle, move the top card to the bottom of the pack. For good measure, do a riffle shuffle, making sure you keep the chosen card at the bottom of the pack.

● Now ask another spectator to choose a number from 1 to 26 and say what that number is.

● Explain what has happened so far: 'I have asked one person to choose a card. I haven't even seen what that card is. I've shuffled the pack thoroughly and then I've asked another person to pick a number from 1 to 26. I didn't know what that number was when I shuffled the pack. Now let's see what happens.'

● Using the glide technique, slide the chosen card back (**1**) and slowly and deliberately deal out cards from the bottom of the pack, face up one at a time, counting them out as you do so.

bottom view

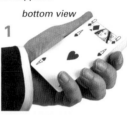

● If, for example, the chosen number was 21, count out 20 cards. When you get to the 21st card, look at the audience and say: 'This is the moment of truth.' As you are doing this, and the audience is momentarily distracted, slide the chosen card forward (**2**) using your little finger. Pick up this card as the 21st card and place it face up. Say: 'Hey presto – the chosen card!'

2

THREE CARDS ACROSS

This is a classic trick involving two spectators and some skilful sleight of hand.

EFFECT

One spectator counts out 15 cards into the performer's hand, then takes the cards and places them in her pocket. Another spectator does the same and places 15 cards in his pocket. The performer then makes three cards travel from one spectator's pocket to the other's. The spectators find that one has 12 cards and the other 18!

EQUIPMENT

A new or nearly new pack of playing cards.

PREPARATION

This trick uses the palm technique (*see page 25*).

PERFORMING

● Ask two spectators to assist you. Get them to stand on either side of you, facing the audience.

● Have one of your assistants shuffle the pack.

1

● Take the pack and hold it in your left hand as if to deal.

● Explain to your assistants what you want them to do, and while you are doing this, move the top three cards to the right (**1**) with your left thumb, and move your little finger under the third card.

● Move your right hand over the pack as though you are squaring the cards, and as you do so, push the cards up with your little finger and close your right hand around them (2).

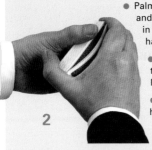

● Palm these three cards and keep them hidden in your relaxed right hand.

● Hand the pack to the spectator on your left.

● Offer her your hand palm up and ask her to count, out loud, 15 cards onto your left hand.

● As the 15th card is counted, turn to the other spectator and say: 'I'll be with you in a moment.' As you turn, bring both hands together and drop the palmed cards from the right hand onto the pile in the left.

● Make as if to square the cards, and then give the 15 cards (really 18) to the first spectator and get her to put them in her pocket.

● Take back the pack and hand it to the second spectator with the request that he, too, count 15 cards onto your left hand.

● As soon as he has counted 12 cards into your hand, move the tip of your little finger over the edge of the top card, so that the last three cards are placed on top, with a small break under them (3).

3

- Ask the second spectator whether he has a suitable pocket in which to put the cards, and as you do so, palm off the three cards into your right hand.

- Again, pretend to square the cards and then hand the cards (now only 12) to him and take back the remainder of the pack in your left hand.

- Bring the right hand across to pick up the pack, and as you do so, drop the palmed cards on top of the pack. Put the pack to one side or in your pocket.

- Now, announce that you are going to make three cards travel from the second spectator's pocket to the first spectator's pocket.

- With a big show, point across from one pocket to the other and say: 'One, two, three!'

- Finish by asking the second spectator to take out his cards and count them onto your right hand – there will be only 12.

- Then ask the first spectator to count her cards onto your left hand – there will be 18!

MIDNIGHT FEAST

This is a trick with a storyline – change it to suit your audience.

EFFECT
One spectator picks a card; another spectator picks a number. The performer then proceeds to find the chosen card at that number place in the pack.

EQUIPMENT
A new or nearly new pack of playing cards.

PREPARATION
Prearrange the pack with any three cards at the top followed by four Js or Qs. You will need to practise the double lift technique (*see page 23*).

PERFORMING

● Explain that this trick is one you learnt one summer holiday when you were young. You and your friends were staying in a large old house, but you were in separate rooms and you wanted to meet up for a midnight feast.

● While you are explaining this, use the lift technique to lift off the four top cards as one (**1**).

● Hold the fourth card toward the audience and explain: 'This card is me.' The audience will think you are holding only one card in your hand.

● Continue: 'After lights out we all arranged to meet in an empty room at the top of the house. These are my friends.' One by one take the next three cards from the top of the pack and add them to the displayed card so that all four cards are visible (2).

2

● 'There we were at the top of the house, tucking into our midnight feast, when we heard a noise outside the door. We all scattered and sneaked back down to our rooms through the fire escape.' As you describe this, take the four Js (or Qs) plus the three hidden cards, square them up and place them face down on top of the pack.

● As you continue with the story, take the top card and, without showing its face, slip it into the pack near the bottom. The next card goes about halfway into the pack and the third card goes about two-thirds of the way from the top. What you have appeared to do is to place the three cards representing your friends randomly in the pack, as if going back to their rooms. What you have actually done is to place three ordinary cards into the pack while leaving the four Js (your friends and you) on top.

● For the finale, say that you waited half an hour until the coast was clear and then made your way up again.

● At this point, turn over the top cards and show the four Js (or Qs).

THE FABULOUS FOUR ACES

This is a classic card trick using a similar technique to that of the previous trick.

EFFECT
The four As are removed from the pack and a spectator chooses her favourite one. The four As are returned to the top of the pack and then dealt into four piles of four cards. Miraculously, all four As are in one pile – the pile the spectator chooses.

EQUIPMENT
A new or nearly new pack of playing cards.

PREPARATION
You will need to practise the double lift (*see page 23*) technique.

PERFORMING
● Openly go through the pack and take out the four As, dropping them face up on the table in any order (**1**).

1

2

● Face a spectator and ask: 'Which one of the aces is your favourite?' As the audience is momentarily distracted, maintain eye contact with the spectator and secretly push the top three cards of the pack slightly to the right, inserting your little finger underneath them to form a break (2).

● Pick up the spectator's favourite A – for example, the A of hearts – and place it face up on top of the pack.

● Place the other three As, also face up, on top of the favourite A.

● With your right hand, bend and lift off the top seven cards (the four face-up As and three face-down cards) (3).

● With the left thumb, scrape the top A to the left, towards the pack in your left hand. The card

3

will still be face up. Name the card and, as you do so, flip your right wrist and hit the back of the A with these cards, flipping the A face down onto the pack (4).

4

● Repeat this procedure with the next two As.

● In your right hand you now have the face-up A of hearts and below it three face-down cards.

● Drop the A of hearts face-up (with cards underneath) onto the pack as though you are handling just one card.

● Pick up the A of hearts and turn it face down on top of the pack, saying: 'And your favourite ace, the ace of hearts.'

● The audience will think the four As are now face down on top of the pack. In reality, there are three other cards between the A of hearts and the other three As.

● Deal the top four cards face down in a row. The first card will be the A of hearts; the others will not be As (5).

5

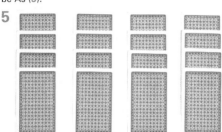

● Then deal three cards on top of each 'A', making sure that the first three cards (the real As) go on top of the A of hearts.

● Now ask a spectator to pick one of the four piles. Use the technique described in The Magician Always Wins (*see page 166*) to force the spectator to arrive at the pile which contains the four As.

● Pick up each of the other piles in turn and deal out the cards to reveal that the piles contain no As. Pause for dramatic effect with each pile before turning over the fourth card and showing it is not an A – the card the audience is expecting to see.

● Finally, deal out the four As in the 'chosen' pile, pausing before dealing out the favourite A as the last card.

5. Tricks using two packs of cards

DO AS I DO

EFFECT
A spectator chooses a card from one pack, and the performer chooses a card from another. They each show the card they have chosen. They are the same!

EQUIPMENT
Two ordinary packs of playing cards with different back designs or colours.

PREPARATION
The two packs must be complete and separate. The trick depends on the use of the glimpse (*see page 22*).

PERFORMING
● Have a spectator choose one pack; you keep the other.

● Tell the volunteer to copy exactly what you do.

● Shuffle your pack, and have the spectator shuffle hers.

● Exchange packs and shuffle the cards again.

● Once again exchange packs, but this time as you square the pack before passing it on, secretly glimpse and remember the bottom card.

● Ask the spectator to remove any card from her pack,

look at it, and remember it, and say that you will do the same. Look at the card you have selected but make no attempt to remember it.

● Each selected card (**a**) is then placed on the top of its pack (**1**) and the packs are then cut once. The selected cards are now 'lost' in their packs. In fact, cutting the spectator's pack has brought the spectator's chosen card (**a**) beneath the card you have glimpsed (**b**).

● Once again, exchange your packs.

● Now ask the spectator to sort through the pack and find the card she chose. Pretend you are doing the same to find the card you chose. In fact, you are hunting for the spectator's card which will be just to the right of the card you glimpsed.

● Remove the card, pretending it is yours, and place it face down. Have the spectator do the same.

● Now explain what you have both done and say: 'Would you be surprised if we both chose the same card?'

● Turn your card over and ask the spectator to do the same. The cards are seen to be the same.

1

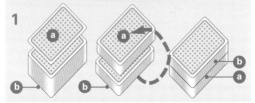

MIRACLE PREDICTION

EFFECT
A spectator freely chooses a card from one pack and discovers it matches the only reversed card in a second pack.

EQUIPMENT
Two ordinary packs of playing cards, in their cases.

PREPARATION
Arrange a card of your choice at the top of one pack. In the other pack, find the same card and turn it over and hide it in the pack. Put the packs back in their cases. If the cases are identical you need to ensure that there is some way to distinguish between them, so that you know which case contains the upside-down card.

PERFORMING
● Place both decks of cards in their cases on the table side by side.

● Ask a spectator to pick one of the decks. If he picks the deck containing the reversed card, ask him to put the deck in his pocket. If he chooses the other deck, keep the deck and put the first deck to one side. Either way, you will be using the deck whose top card you know.

● Take the pack out of the case and ask a spectator to give you a number, somewhere between 1 and 52, adding: 'It's best not to make it too high a number otherwise we could be here all day.'

● Pick up the deck and deal out that number of cards, say 22, counting out loud as you do so (the known card (**a**) is now on the bottom of the dealt pile).

● When you have finished, pretend to change your mind. Say: 'Wait a minute, it's better if you demonstrate the trick.'

● Put the pile of cards on top of the pack. The known card is now twenty-second from the top.

● Hand the pack to the spectator, and ask him to repeat what you did (1) – to count down and deal to number 22. Ask him to place the twenty-second card (**a**) to one side.

● Continue by saying: 'Now remember the other pack? No one has touched it, is that right?' Ask the spectator to take it out of his pocket or pick it up from the table. 'Open it up and you'll see all the cards are the same way up, except for one. What is that card?'

● Then ask the spectator to turn over the twenty-second card. The two cards match!

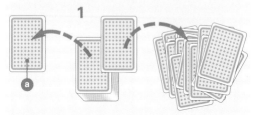

THE RED CARD

This is a novel trick using a stacked sequence of 10 cards from two packs.

EFFECT

The performer writes a prediction on a piece of paper. A spectator then chooses a number from 1 to 10. The performer deals out 10 cards. The spectator discloses her chosen number, and the performer uses the 10 cards to show how her chosen number fulfils the prediction.

EQUIPMENT

Two packs of playing cards – one with a red back design, the other with a back design of a different colour – are needed, as are a piece of paper and a pencil.

PREPARATION

From the red-backed pack, take out any card from a black suit. From the other pack, take out any eight black cards and any red card. Arrange these cards in a stack, alternating face up and face down, so that when you deal them out in a line (**1**) the third card from the left (**a**) has a red back design and the fourth card (**b**) is of a red suit. The actual values of the cards are not important.

1

PERFORMING

● Explain that you are going to write down a prediction. On a piece of paper write: 'You will choose a red card.'

● Fold the paper and hand it to one of the spectators for safekeeping. Do not disclose what you have written.

● Ask a spectator to choose a number from 1 to 10. The number chosen will determine your next move.

● If the chosen number is 1, 2, 5, 6, 9 or 10, spell the number, tapping a card from left to right for each letter as you do so. (Numbers 1, 2, 6 and 10 have three letters and take you to the third card. Numbers 5 and 9 have four letters and so take you to the fourth card.)

● If the chosen number is 3 or 4, simply count along the row from left to right. If the chosen number is 7 or 8, count along the row from right to left.

● Either way, whatever number is chosen, you will end up on either the third or fourth card from the left. Now all you have to do is reveal your prediction.

● If it is the third card, turn all the face-up cards face down. Turn the third card over. It is the only card with a red back.

● If it is the fourth card, turn all the face-down cards face up. The fourth card will be the only red card.

● Ask the spectator to unfold the paper and read out your prediction!

A WORLD RECORD

This is a very impressive trick using a prearranged deck switched with a shuffled one. It requires at least four spectators.

EFFECT
Several spectators each choose a card and replace them anywhere in the pack. The performer then finds them all.

EQUIPMENT
Two ordinary packs of playing cards of identical design, and an elastic band.

PERFORMING
● Explain that this trick was once performed to break a world record.

● Fan the cards face down.

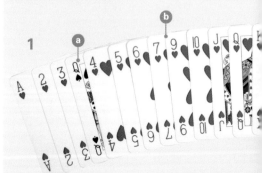

PREPARATION

You will need to practise the false overhand shuffle, keeping the order of the pack (*see page 10*) and switching packs (*see page 27*). Prepare one pack with each suit in order, from A through to K. Place this prearranged pack in your pocket. When you have finished an earlier trick using the other pack, get a spectator to shuffle it well and then swap the two decks in your pocket (as described at switching packs) before performing this trick.

● Ask each spectator to come forward, take a card, remember it, and then return it anywhere in the pack.

● When all the spectators have done this, close the fan and do a false overhand shuffle to cut the cards once or twice, but maintain the order.

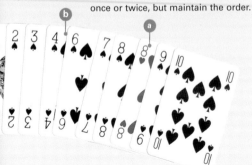

● Turn the pack to face yourself, and ask everyone to think hard of the card they chose. Explain how difficult the trick is, and how you need all the help you can get.

● Look through the cards (**1**, see previous page). It should be easy to spot cards which are out of sequence (**a**). Don't forget there will be gaps where cards have been removed (**b**).

● As you come to each card out of sequence, take it out and throw it face down on the table, but leave one of the chosen cards in the pack. Remember this card.

● Explain that one of the spectators isn't concentrating properly, and say that you know who it is.

● Now riffle shuffle the pack two or three times to really mix up the arrangement.

● Look through the pack a final time and say: 'That's better.' Take out the final card and put it with the rest.

● Now pick up all the selected cards – there should be one for each spectator.

● Hold the cards toward you. Ask each spectator, in turn, to name her or his card. As each does so, throw it out face up on the table.

● When you have finished, say: 'Back in the 18th century, [give the number of spectators] was a record for the number of cards identified in a single trick.'

● Finish by spreading the pack face up to demonstrate that the cards are not in any order.

POCKET PREDICTION

EFFECT

The spectator takes one pack, the performer another, and
both packs are well shuffled. The performer removes one
card from her face-down pack and pushes it into the
spectator's right-hand jacket pocket. The spectator selects
a card from his face-down pack and puts it into the
performer's right-hand jacket pocket. The performer
summarises what has happened so far and then removes
the card from her pocket. The spectator removes the card
from his. The cards are identical.

EQUIPMENT

Two ordinary packs of playing cards of different back
design or colour. You will also need two jackets with deep
side pockets – one for you and one for the spectator.

PREPARATION

From one pack remove a known card (**a**) and place it in
your jacket pocket (**1**) lying horizontally with the back
facing outwards.

Place the identical card
in the other pack at the
top of that pack; it is
the key card. You will
need to practise the
false overhand shuffle
(*see page 10*).

PERFORMING

● Place the two packs face down on the table, side by side. Ask the spectator to pick a pack. If he picks the pack containing the key card, tell him to put that pack to one side. He should then pick up the remaining pack. If he picks the pack without the key card, let him keep it. Either way, he is left with the pack without the key card.

● Ask him to shuffle the pack thoroughly using an overhand shuffle. As he does this, say that you will do the same.

● Take the other pack and use a false overhand shuffle to keep the top card in place.

● Ask the spectator to take a card from his pack and, without looking at it, put the card in your right-hand jacket pocket.

Note: *The card is bound to go in vertically rather than horizontally, and so you will not confuse it with your hidden card.*

● Say that you will do the same. At this point simply take your top card and without showing it to anyone put it in the spectator's pocket.

● Summarise what has happened so far and finish by saying: 'I wonder what the chances are of us both choosing the same card – about 50 to 1, I suppose.' With that, ask the spectator to take the card out of his pocket. You do the same, making sure you take out the horizontal card (**a**).

● You both place your cards face up on the table. They match!

6. Card novelties

This chapter contains a potpourri of tricks, puzzles and oddities. Some are card tricks; others are strange properties that the cards themselves possess. Sprinkle these novelties among the more traditional card tricks elsewhere in this book to keep the audience entertained.

SPELLING THE PACK

This is an alternative way of checking that there are the correct number of cards in the pack.

EFFECT
Count the cards by 'spelling' them from A through to K. The number of letters gives you the number 52.

EQUIPMENT
An ordinary pack of 52 playing cards.

PREPARATION
No preparation is required.

PERFORMING
● Simply deal the cards face down, spelling out the names of all the cards in a suit (A to K) and dealing one card for each letter. Start by spelling out A (three cards: 'a-c-e'), and dealing out three cards; then spell out 2 (three cards: 't-w-o'), 3 (five cards: 't-h-r-e-e') and so on, through to the K (4 cards: 'k-i-n-g').

● Done correctly, the fifty-second card dealt will fall on the 'g' of 'king' (*see page 157*).

Note: *This also works if you 'spell' the pack in French.*

English			French	
ace	3		as	2
two	3		deux	4
three	5		trois	5
four	4		quatre	6
five	4		cinq	4
six	3		six	3
seven	5		sept	4

English			French	
eight	5		huit	4
nine	4		neuf	4
ten	3		dix	3
jack	4		valet	5
queen	5		reine	5
king	4		roi	3
Total	**52**		**Total**	**52**

THE CARD CALENDAR

This is a good opener for other tricks.

1

EFFECT
The performer tells a simple story showing how the standard card pack is designed around the calendar year – days and nights, the four seasons, 13 lunar months, 52 weeks and 365 days.

EQUIPMENT
An ordinary pack of playing cards with jokers.

PREPARATION
Keep the two jokers to one side. Arrange the rest of the pack into four piles, each containing a suit in order from A through to K. Re-form the pack by putting the four piles in order, starting with a red suit on top and alternating with a black suit (**1**).

PERFORMING

● Start with the pack face down in your hand.

● Begin the story by saying: 'Did you know that the first pack of cards was designed by a wizard, living at a time when people were much more in touch with nature?'

● Continue: 'One of the things he tried to do was show how his cards reflected nature.'

● 'The red cards represented the sun and daytime, the black cards darkness and night-time.' Show the top card (red) and the bottom card (black). Then replace the cards in their original positions.

● 'The four suits represented the four seasons of the year.' Cut the pack into four piles of 13 cards and place the piles face up.

● 'The number of cards in each suit is 13, the number of lunar months in a year. A lunar month is about 28 days.' Spread one of the suits to show the 13 cards.

● 'The number of cards in the pack is 52, the number of weeks in the year.'

● 'And last but not least, if you count the total number of spots on the cards (taking J as 11, Q as 12 and K as 13) you get 364. Add a single joker, and you get 365, the number of days in the year. Add both jokers, and you get 366, the number of days in a leap year. This wizard knew what he was doing.'

● Scoop up the cards and give the pack two or three riffle shuffles. You are now ready to do your first trick.

BOMB AIMING

EFFECT
When a spectator tries to drop a card into a hat she can't.
The performer can do it every time.

EQUIPMENT
An ordinary pack of 52 playing cards and an empty hat
or wastepaper bin.

PREPARATION
Practise 'bomb aiming' so that you can do it accurately
each and every time.

● To 'bomb aim' a card, gently hold the card
lengthwise between thumb and middle finger (1).

● Hold the card so that it is absolutely horizontal and
move it into position over the target.

● Carefully sight the card so that you release it
directly over the centre of the target.

PERFORMING

● Place the wastepaper bin or hat open end up on the floor (2).

● Challenge a spectator to drop a card from chest height and get it in the hat or bin five times out of five.

● The spectator is very unlikely to succeed because she doesn't know the technique.

● Then take the same card and 'bomb aim' it into the hat or bin five times. You should be able to drop the card into the hat or bin each time.

● When you have finished, you can choose to show the spectator the technique, or leave her to stew and try it again another day.

2

A CARD PUZZLE

This is a quick and simple puzzle to use any time in a performance.

EFFECT
The challenge for the spectators is to find a quick solution to a puzzle involving three cards. It's not as easy as it looks.

EQUIPMENT
An ordinary pack of 52 playing cards.

PREPARATION
Make sure you know the answer before performing this one.

PERFORMING
● Deal three cards face down in a row on the table in front of several spectators.

● Ask each spectator to turn the centre card of his or her row of three face up. This is the start position (1).

● The rules of the puzzle are as follows: Each move involves turning over two cards. The challenge is – in exactly three moves, no more and no less – to finish with all three cards face up.

1

● Give the spectators a couple of minutes to try. After each attempt they can reset the cards to the start position and try again.

● If one of the spectators thinks he has found the answer, take him to one side to demonstrate it to you.

● When the two minutes is up, you (or the successful spectator) can demonstrate to the others how the trick is done.

● The solution is shown here (2) (the mirror image of this solution will work too):

2

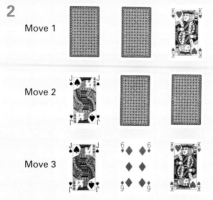

Move 1

Move 2

Move 3

Move 1: turn over the second and third card.
Move 2: turn over the first and third card.
Move 3: turn over the second and third card.

ANOTHER CARD PUZZLE

This is another simple puzzle using three cards.

EFFECT
The spectators must decipher written clues to arrive at the correct solution.

EQUIPMENT
An ordinary pack of playing cards, a pencil and paper.

PERFORMING
● Deal the three top cards face down in a row on the table (**1**).

● Explain: 'The cards are numbered 1 to 3 from left to right. To find the solution you have to unravel this information.' Place the paper in front of the spectators and read out the clues.

1

PREPARATION

Write out the following on the piece of paper: 'There is at least one 3 to the right of a 2. There is at least one 3 to the left of a 3. There is at least one heart to the left of a club. There is at least one heart to the right of a heart. What are the three cards?' Sort through the pack of cards and arrange the three cards as follows: 2 of hearts, 3 of hearts and 3 of clubs in order at the top of the pack.

● Leave the paper there so that the spectators can refer to it.

● Give the spectators two minutes, and offer a prize to see who can come up with the solution first.

● When someone has the answer, or time has run out, turn over the cards (2) and show the correct solution.

2

THE MAGICIAN ALWAYS WINS

This provides quick entertainment at any time in a performance and enhances your reputation as a magician.

EFFECT
A spectator is apparently given a free choice of three cards. The performer will always correctly predict which is the chosen card.

EQUIPMENT
An ordinary pack of 52 playing cards.

PREPARATION
Practise the patter so that you can perform the trick quickly and without having to think about what to say.

PERFORMING
● Fan the cards with the faces towards you.

● Remove an A and place it face down on the table to one side (1), adding: 'This card predicts what will happen.'

● Continue looking through the cards and pull out any two cards and one

1

other A. Remember where this A is located among the three cards and place the three cards face down on the table (2).

2

● Say: 'Here are three cards. Pick up any two of them.' What happens next depends on which cards the spectator chooses.

● If she leaves behind the A (whose location you will have memorised), the trick is over. In that case say: 'I predicted you would leave the ace', and simply turn over the other A that you had set aside earlier.

● If she picks up the A as one of her two chosen cards, ask her to hand you one of her cards. If she gives you the A, respond with: 'There was a one-in-three chance that you would give me the ace. And you have.' Then turn over your set-aside A to prove your prediction was right.

● If, after handing you one of her two cards, the spectator is left with the A in her hands, simply say: 'You have kept the ace. I predicted you would,' and turn over your set-aside A.

● Whatever happens, the magician always wins.

FOUR-CARD INDEX

EFFECT
The spectator thinks of a card. The performer asks what the card is, then delves into a pocket and, without looking, takes out, in the right order, up to four cards which depict the card's value and suit.

EQUIPMENT
An ordinary pack of 52 playing cards and a jacket with deep side pockets.

PREPARATION
Arrange the following four cards in number sequence, with the A on top: A of clubs, 2 of hearts, 4 of spades and the 8 of diamonds (1). Remember their order. This is easily done, because each card is double the value of the one before. The order of suits is remembered using the word CHaSeD (see page 87). Place the cards horizontally in your pocket, with the backs facing out.

Set the remainder of
the pack aside.

1

PERFORMING

● Ask a spectator to shuffle the pack and then think of any card.

● Take back the pack and place the cards vertically in your pocket behind the four horizontal cards already there.

● Continue: 'I haven't yet reached the stage where I can take out your card without looking for it. But at the very least I can take out some cards which are equivalent to it. Let me show you.'

● Say to the spectator: 'Name your card.' No matter what card is named, you can make up the combination using the four cards from your pocket. Whichever suit is chosen, you can show as the first or last card you lay down. The values of the cards can be made to add up to any number between 1 and 13.

● Two examples are shown (2), overleaf.

● Think before dipping your hand into your pocket. Try to come up with the best combination to illustrate the chosen card. By placing a finger between each of the four horizontal cards, you should be able to pick up cleanly the precise cards you need, each and every time.

● In rare cases, someone's chosen card will be one of your four. Then you have a real miracle!

2 Spectator chooses the 5 of hearts

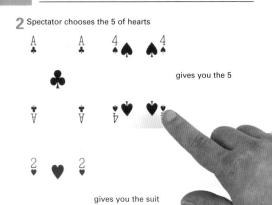

gives you the 5

gives you the suit

Spectator chooses the J of clubs (value 11)

adds up to 11; the first card gives the suit

YOU BET

EFFECT
The performer places a coin on a card and balances the
card on a finger. The performer then challenges a
spectator to remove the card without touching the coin,
and to leave the coin balanced on the finger. The spectator
tries and fails. The performer shows how it is done.

EQUIPMENT
A single card from a new or nearly new deck and a ten-
pence or one-pound coin.

PREPARATION
Practise the technique, so you can do it every time.

● The coin needs to be exactly in place over the ball of
your finger.

● Flick the index finger of your right hand against the
edge at one end of the card.

● The card should fly through the air, leaving the coin
balanced on your finger.

PERFORMING
● Balance a playing card on the ball of your index
finger (1, overleaf).

● Carefully position a ten-pence or one-pound coin on
the card directly over the ball of the finger.

● Challenge the spectators by saying: 'I'm willing to
bet that I can remove the card and leave the coin
balanced on my finger.'

- Allow a spectator to try it a few times. Without knowing the technique, the spectator is likely to fail each time.

- With a flourish, show how it is done (2).

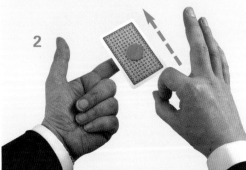

STEPPING THROUGH A CARD

EFFECT
The performer challenges the onlookers by claiming to be able to step through a card, then proceeding to do so.

EQUIPMENT
An ordinary pack of playing cards and an additional card that you are willing to damage, such as a joker or an instruction card, plus a pair of scissors.

PREPARATION
Prepare the card (**1**) by first cutting a slit in it lengthwise along its centre (**a**), leaving a 3–4 mm thickness of card intact at both ends (**b**).

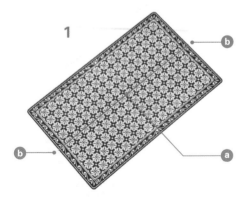

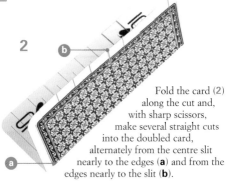

Fold the card (**2**) along the cut and, with sharp scissors, make several straight cuts into the doubled card, alternately from the centre slit nearly to the edges (**a**) and from the edges nearly to the slit (**b**).

Flatten the card so that it is back to its original shape, and then hide the card in the pack (**3**). It will make an obvious gap in the pack and so will be easy to locate.

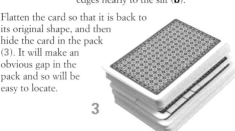

PERFORMING

● Begin by saying: 'Have you ever seen a performer step through a playing card? Impossible? Oh, no it's not. Here's one I prepared earlier.'

● Riffle through the pack and take out your prepared card. Slowly and carefully, and with maximum suspense, open up the card into a large zigzag loop (4).

● Step through the loop, and then take a deep bow.

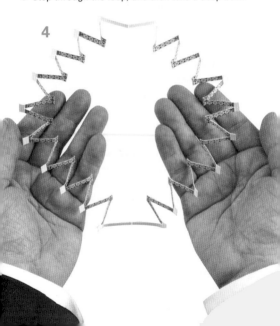

4

SIX-CARD LIFT

EFFECT

The performer challenges the spectators to arrange six
cards in such a way that lifting one card lifts all the others,
while the faces of all the cards remain visible. When the
spectators fail to do this, the performer shows how it's
done.

EQUIPMENT

Six cards from an ordinary pack of playing cards.

PREPARATION

Practise the technique so that you can quickly and easily
show how it is done. The arranging technique is as follows:

● Place the first card (1) – the master card – face down
vertically on the table in front of you.

● Place the next card (2) horizontally on top.

● The remaining four cards (3–6) are tucked in around
the first two. This is done by placing two cards (3 and
4) tucked horizontally behind the master card.

● The last two (5 and 6) are placed vertically, tucked
over card 2 and behind cards 3 and 4.

● The arrangement can be lifted up by card 2 and
turned over to show the faces of the cards.

PERFORMING

● Spread six cards on the table face down.

● Challenge the spectators to come up with a way of
arranging the cards so that they can lift all six cards

by holding only one card by its edges. There is a further snag – all the faces of the cards must be visible when the cards are lifted.

● When the spectators have tried and, most likely, failed, show how it is done.

CARD THROUGH THE HOLE

This is a very adaptable trick that is particularly suitable for a young audience.

EFFECT

The performer asks a member of the audience to push a card through a small hole without bending the card. When the spectator fails to do this, the performer shows how. If the spectator discovers the technique and is able to perform the trick, the performer can nevertheless complete the trick in style, with a humorous flourish.

EQUIPMENT

A standard-size playing card, a 10 cm square of thin card, a modelling knife and cutting board, a drawing compass and a pencil.

PREPARATION

Using the compass, draw a circle 3.75 cm wide in the centre of the card square. Cut out the circle using the knife on the board, so that you are left with a hole in the centre of the card (1). Have the card square, the playing card and the pencil to hand when you start the trick.

PERFORMING

● Challenge a spectator to push the playing card through the hole in the square without bending the playing card or tearing the card square.

● When he fails, as is likely, show him how the trick is done.

● Fold the card square in half (2) and then gently bend down the edges at the fold, so that the hole opens wider (3).

● Done carefully, the hole widens until it is big enough for the playing card to be pushed through (4, overleaf).

● To finish with a light touch (or as a backup should the spectator succeed), finish with: 'Of course, there is another way to do the trick.'

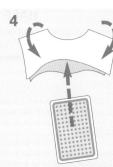

● Pick up the pencil and push it through the hole in the card so that it touches the playing card (5). Add: 'See, I am pushing the card through the hole!'

HALF CUT

This is a self-working card trick using half cards. The pack, prepared in advance, can be carried easily in a pocket and used anytime, anywhere.

EFFECT

By a random process, two spectators each select a half card from a pack of half cards. It is later revealed that they have the two halves of the same card.

EQUIPMENT

An ordinary pack of playing cards (an old pack, which you won't mind destroying), a metal rule, a modelling knife and cutting board, and a pencil.

PREPARATION

Take 17 cards from the pack. Choose cards of all four suits and of assorted values (1).

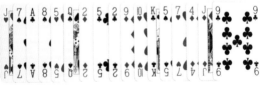

1

Take the metal rule and, with a pencil, lightly mark each card at the centre of each long edge (2).

2

Carefully cut across the centre of each of the 17 cards using the modelling knife on a cutting board. You will be left with 34 half cards.

Arrange these cards with their cut edges aligned.

PERFORMING

● Shuffle the pack of half cards, making sure to keep the cut edges aligned. Offer the face-down pack to one spectator, explaining: 'This pack was formed from ordinary cards which were cut in half. Check them if you like.'

● Now have the spectator put the pack face down on the table and lift off and keep a portion of the cards.

● Have another spectator pick up the remaining cards.

● Ask the two spectators to silently count their cards while your back is turned and to memorise the number.

● Still with your back turned, ask the second spectator to give her cards to the first spectator, who then shuffles the two piles together.

● Turn around, take the cards, and deal them one at a time face up towards the first spectator. Ask him to mentally count the cards as they are shown and to remember the particular card that falls at the number he had earlier memorised. Tell him to give no visible indication – either to you or the other spectator – of his number or the card.

● The essence of the trick lies in the way you show

the cards to the spectator. Hold the cards in your left hand, facing towards the first spectator.

● Push off the top card with your left thumb and take it in your right hand, with its face still towards the first spectator.

● Then push off the next card with your thumb and

show it to the first spectator as you transfer it to your right hand behind the first card (3).

● Continue in this way with all the cards so that you reverse the order of the cards.

● When you get to the last card, show the card to the spectator but then keep the card face down in your left hand and place all the other cards on top of it (4).

● Now turn to the second spectator. Ask

her to count the cards mentally as you transfer them, face up and one at a time, from your left hand to your right, and ask her to remember the particular card that falls at the number she had earlier memorised. Tell her to give no visible indication of her number or the card.

● Hold the cards in your left hand, facing the spectator, as you did before.

● Proceed to show the second spectator all the cards, one at a time, as you transfer them to your right hand as before. This time, however, there is one important difference. When you get to the last card in your left hand put it on top of the face-down cards in your right hand (5).

5

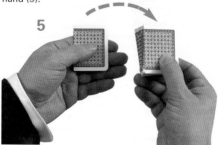

● When finished, hand the face-down pack to the first spectator, get him to shuffle them and then instruct him to find his particular card, which he is to place face down on the table.

● Ask the first spectator to hand the pack to the second, who now sorts through to find her card, which she places face down on the table.

● Place the two cut ends of the cards together (6) and quickly run through what has happened: 'The pack was shuffled; you both had a random number of cards – only you knew how many; you used this number to later select a card.'

6

● Look at the first spectator and, pointing to his half card, say: 'This is your half, is it not?' Then look at the second spectator and, pointing to her half, say: 'This is yours.'

● 'What is remarkable is that they are both from the same card!' Turn over the halves and it will be seen that they are matching halves of the same card (7)!

7

Note: *The trick works on the simple premise that the two numbers must add up to 34. If one spectator's number is 16, for example, the other's must be 18. The rest is determined by the way the cards are shown to the spectators.*

FOUR ACES

EFFECT
The performer magically extracts the four As by dealing from a face-down deck of cards.

EQUIPMENT
An old pack of playing cards that you do not mind marking.

PREPARATION
Use a pin or needle to scratch away some of the back design on the top left of the four As (**a**). Mix them in with the rest of the pack (**1**).

1

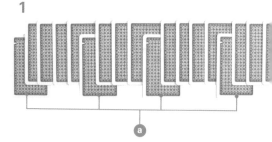

a

PERFORMING
● Shuffle the pack using an overhand shuffle.

● Explain to onlookers: 'Few people know that the aces carry less printing ink than the other cards, and so weigh less. With practice you can feel this.'

● Slowly deal out the cards face down. As you do so, make a show of pretending to weigh each card, but actually look for the marked ones.

● Deal all the unmarked cards (2) into one pile (a), and the four marked cards into a separate pile (b).

2

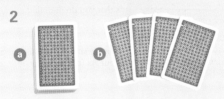

● When you have finished, pick up the four separate cards. Spread them out face up on the table to show the spectators that they are the four As (3).

3

● When you have finished, put them under the other cards so the spectators will not notice how the trick was done.

FIND THE CARD

EFFECT
The performer cuts a shuffled pack into two piles. The
spectator chooses a card from one pile, remembers it and
places it in the other pile. The performer shuffles the two
piles together and extracts the chosen card.

EQUIPMENT
Mark all the cards in a pack as described on page 186 to
give a marked one-way desk.

PREPARATION
Prepare the pack by placing all the cards with their backs
the same way up (1).

1

PERFORMING
● Shuffle the pack using an overhand shuffle.

● Cut the pack into two equal piles, but reverse one
pile so that its back design is upside down (2).

● Ask a spectator to select a card from one pile, look
at it, and replace it in the other pile.

2

● Turn the first pile the right way up and riffle shuffle the two piles together.

● Spread the deck face down (3) in a ribbon spread (*see page 16*). The chosen card will be the one which is upside down (**a**). Quickly remove it from the row of cards. Make a big show of finding the card, exclaiming 'Here it is!' and engaging in lively patter as you show it to the spectators to confirm that it is the chosen card. By doing so, you distract the audience away from noticing that the card backs are marked.

3   **a**

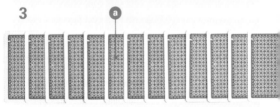

● When you are finished, return the card, right side up, to the row of cards. Quickly square the pack and begin a new trick with a different pack of cards.

FINALE

This is a good way of finishing your routine – but you will
be destroying a deck of cards in the process!

EFFECT

The performer asks the strongest spectator to tear the
pack of cards in half. Providing the pack is kept tightly
together, and the cards are not separated, the spectator is
likely to fail. The performer then takes back the pack and
tears it in half.

EQUIPMENT

Two well-used packs of linen-backed playing cards of the
same design (one of which you are willing to destroy), an
elastic band and a jacket with deep side pockets. You also
will need a sharp modelling knife and cutting board or a
hot oven, heatproof plates and oven gloves.

Note: *Adult supervision is needed if oven is used.*

PREPARATION

Prepare one of the packs of cards for tearing. There are
two ways of doing this.

● Spread the cards out on clean plates and place them
in an oven at 140 °C (gas mark 1) for about 90 minutes.
Use oven gloves to lift out the plates and allow the cards
to cool to room temperature. They will now be dry and
brittle, and easily torn, so handle them carefully.

● Alternatively, with great care, make a 2 cm-deep cut
in one side of 50 cards in the pack (**a**). Hide the cut by
placing the two uncut cards (**b**) at top and bottom of
the pack (**1**).

Prepare the packs for switching (*see page 27*), with the prepared pack in your pocket held together by an elastic band. The normal pack is in your hand.

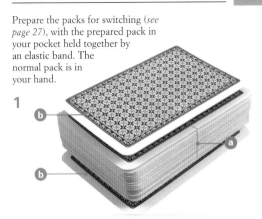

1

b

a

b

PERFORMING

● Pick out the strongest-looking member of your audience and ask him or her to tear the pack in half, but keeping the pack tightly together, not separating the cards. Give the spectator about a minute to perform the task.

● It is likely that some of the cards will be slightly mangled or dog-eared, but the spectator won't actually be able to tear the pack in half.

● Take the pack back, shuffle it and say: 'We'll leave it for another day.' Put the pack in your pocket and as you do so, switch over the two packs of cards. Then suddenly appear to change your mind and say: 'OK. I'll show you how it's done.'

● Bring out the 'treated' pack of cards and proceed to tear it in half. There is a different method depending on how you have treated the cards.

● If you have cut the cards with a knife, tear them by twisting the pack. Do not show the pieces to the spectators – they will see the cut.

● If you have baked the cards, grip the pack tightly at both ends and flex the pack up and down until the pack splits in half (2).

● Put the card pieces in your pocket, take a bow and leave.

2

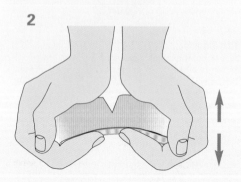

COLLINS GEM
1950s
a mine of information

COLLINS GEM
1960s
a mine of information

COLLINS GEM
1970s
a mine of information

COLLINS GE
1980
a mine of information

COLLINS   Jane's
CIVIL AIRCRAFT
a mine of information

COLLINS GEM
CLANS & Tartans
a mine of information

COLLINS GEM
Classic
TV SERIES
a mine of information

COLLINS   Jane
COMBAT AIRCRAF
a mine of information

COLLINS GEM
FIRSTS
a mine of information

COLLINS GEM
GOLF
a mine of information

COLLINS GEM
HILLWALKER'S Survival Guide
a mine of information

COLLINS GE
HOME EMERGENCY GUID
a mine of information

COLLINS GEM
Collecting
STAMPS
a mine of information

COLLINS GEM
STARS
a mine of information

COLLINS GEM
SUPERSTITIONS
a mine of information

COLLINS GE
Using Your
SOFTWAR
a mine of information